MBA QUICK BOOK FOR MINISTERS

VINCENT WYATT HOWELL &
VINCENT WYATT HOWELL JR.

JUDSON PRESS

PUBLISHERS SINCE 1824

VALLEY FORGE, PA

MBA Quick Book for Ministers
© 2019 by Judson Press, Valley Forge, PA 19482-0851
All rights reserved.

Judson Press has made every effort to trace the ownership of all quotes. In the event of a question arising from the use of a quote, we regret any error made and will be pleased to make the necessary correction in future printings and editions of this book.

Bible quotations in this volume are from the Contemporary English Version. Copyright © 1991, 1992, 1995 by American Bible Society. Used by permission. (CEV); The Holy Bible, English Standard Version. Copyright © 2001 by Crossway Bibles, a publishing ministry of Good News Publishers. (ESV); *The Holy Bible*, King James Version (KJV); The Living Bible copyright © 1971 by Tyndale House Foundation. Used by permission of Tyndale House Publishers Inc., Carol Stream, Illinois 60188. All rights reserved. (TLB); the New American Standard Bible, © 1960, 1962, 1963, 1968, 1971, 1972, 1973, 1975, 1977 by The Lockman Foundation. Used by permission. (NASB); HOLY BIBLE, New International Version®, NIV®, copyright © 1973, 1978, 1984, 2011 by Biblica Inc. Used by permission. All rights reserved worldwide. (NIV); The New King James Version. Copyright © 1972, 1984 by Thomas Nelson Inc. (NKJV); the New Revised Standard Version of the Bible, copyright © 1989 by the Division of Christian Education of the National Council of the Churches of Christ in the United States of America. Used by permission. All rights reserved. (NRSV).

Interior design by Wendy Ronga, Hampton Design Group.
Cover design by Danny Ellison.

Library of Congress Cataloging-in-Publication data
Names: Howell, Vincent Wyatt, author. | Howell, Vincent Wyatt, Jr., author.
Title: MBA quick book for ministers / Vincent Wyatt Howell and Vincent Wyatt Howell, Jr.
Description: Valley Forge, PA: Judson Press, [2019] | Includes bibliographical references.
Identifiers: LCCN 2019010983 (print) | LCCN 2019016644 (ebook) | ISBN 9780817082031 (epub) | ISBN 9780817018078 (pbk.: alk. paper) Subjects: LCSH: Church management. | Church personnel management. | Christian leadership. Classification: LCC BV652 (ebook) | LCC BV652 .H68 2019 (print) | DDC 254—dc23 LC record available at https://lccn.loc.gov/2019010983

Printed in the U.S.A.

First printing, 2019.

To my loving wife, Carolyn,
my partner in life and ministry,
who has been my cheerleader and encourager
throughout the years in ministry;
to my two wonderful children, Naila and Vincent Jr.;
my daughter-in-law, LaToya; and my two
beautiful grandchildren.
I give thanks to Christ my Savior,
and I honor the memory of our parents,
the late William and Lillian Howell and the late
Herbert and Carrie Kelley,
and my older brother, the late William Howell, Jr.

VINCENT W. HOWELL

To LaToya, Vincent III, and Camryn,
my inspiration and my motivation.
Thank you for your endless love and support.

VINCENT W. HOWELL JR.

Contents

Illustrations

Preface

Look at any of the recent research on church attendance, and you, the reader, will note that times have changed. Many mainline churches show little or no statistical growth (for example, numerical or new professions of faith), and many have minimal impact on the surrounding communities. Instead of looking for innovation and breakthroughs in making disciples for Christ for the transformation of the world, too many struggle and focus on just keeping their doors open. Coupled with that, too many churches across the country are slowly dying because they look to traditions of the past instead of using pastoral leadership capacity to expand God's reach—because people still need Christ!

Elmer L. Towns, Ed Stetzer, and Warren Bird, authors of *Eleven Innovations in the Local Church*, make a critical observation about the need for innovation in leadership strategy: "The message to us all is this: When culture changes, adjust your methods or you will lose your effectiveness . . . but never change your message or your principles! When methods no longer work, don't blame the harvest as being unreachable; instead, ask God if it's time to change your methods!"[1]

Statistics point to a need for a paradigm shift in pastoral leadership. In *Outreach Magazine's* April 10, 2018 article "7 Startling Facts: An Up Close Look at Church Attendance in America," researchers make five key points.[2]

> 1. Fewer than 20 percent of Americans regularly attend church—half of what the pollsters report.
> 2. American church attendance is steadily declining. "Church researcher and author Thom Rainer notes that

the failure of churches to keep up with the population growth is one of the church's greatest issues heading into the future. In a 2002 survey of 1,159 U.S. churches, Rainer's research team found that only 6 percent of the churches were growing—he defines growth as not only increasing in attendance, but also increasing at a pace faster than its community's population growth rate. "Stated inversely, 94 percent of our churches are losing ground in the communities they served," he says.

3. Only one state [Hawaii] is outpacing its population growth.

4. Mid-sized churches are shrinking; the smallest and largest churches are growing, . . . During [1994 to 2004], the smallest churches grew 16.4 percent; the largest grew 21.5 percent, exceeding the national population growth of 12.2 percent. But mid-sized churches (100–299)—the average size of a Protestant church in America is 124—declined 1 percent.

5. Established churches—40 to 190 years old—are, on average, declining.

6. The increase in churches is only ¼ of what's needed to keep up with population growth. Between 2000 and 2004, the net gain (the number of new churches minus the closed churches) in the number of evangelical churches was 5,452, but mainline and Catholic churches closed more than they started for a net loss of 2,200, leaving an overall net gain of 3,252 for all Orthodox Christian churches. . . . In the 21st century, the net gain in churches has amounted to only 800 each year.[2]

7. In 2050, the percentage of the U.S. population attending church will be almost half of what it was in 1990.

Are these statistics a cause for panic? We would contend that the answer is no! These statistics point to a clear need for a new leadership paradigm for pastors as they serve as chief executives for making disciples for Christ.

One way that pastors can build strong leadership and management skills to support theological education is to pursue the Master of Business Administration (MBA) degree. In researching this book, we found evidence that supports this contention. Several seminaries currently offer a joint Master of Divinity/Master of Business Administration degree (see appendix 1 for a sample list).

Realizing that all pastors are not in a position to return to school, we designed this book to give pastors insight into important MBA topics that can benefit pastoral leadership. In addition, we will share wisdom from pastors who have completed this degree in order to enhance pastoral leadership. By so doing, it is our hope that our journey as pastors will be one of continuing leadership education, thereby helping us in "the equipping of the saints for the work of ministry, for the edifying of the body of Christ, till we all come to the unity of the faith and of the knowledge of the Son of God" (Ephesians 4:12-13a, NKJV).

Notes

1. Elmer L. Towns, Ed Stetzer, and Warren Bird, "The Church Changed, and Nobody Told Us," Crosswalk, http://www.cross walk.com/church/pastors-or-leadership/the-church-changed-and-nobody-told-us-11562925.html, adapted from *Eleven Innovations in the Local Church* (Ventura, CA: Regal, 2007).

2. *Outreach Magazine*, "7 Startling Facts: An Up Close Look at Church Attendance in America," April 10, 2018, ChurchLeaders, http://churchleaders.com/pastors/pastor-articles/139575-7-star tling-facts-an-up-close-look-at-church-attendance-in-america.html.

Acknowledgments

One of the things I have learned in life and in ministry is that leadership is a team effort. It is this idea of team that has continued to influence me in writing and service to our Lord and Savior Jesus Christ. During these past eight years, I have had the wonderful experience of serving with some inspirational pastors and lay leaders. When serving in the Upper New York Annual Conference of the United Methodist Church, I had the opportunity to share my leadership skill and insight on various district and conference committees. These experiences continue to reinforce the importance of leadership on church vitality and discipleship making. For this experience, I thank Rev. Nancy Adams, District Superintendent of the Mountain View District, and Bishop Mark Webb, Resident Bishop of the Upper New York Conference of the United Methodist Church. These experiences have been foundational in my leadership development. Thank you.

Lay leadership in so critical in the church of today as we pastors seek to share and implement the vision Christ has put on our hearts. This vision process is greatly influenced by the opportunity to share and dialogue. My leadership insight has benefited in this regard from many church leadership conversations with Arthur Q. Thompson of Westside United Methodist Church and Ann Welch-Wood of Webb Mills United Methodist Church. Thank you.

As a pastor who has served in both the United Methodist Church and the African Methodist Episcopal Zion Church, I am grateful to the people of my home church, Wardell Chapel AME Zion Church, Shelby, North Carolina, for their early nurturing. And to all the churches I have served in Lackawanna, New York; Ithaca, New York, Rochester, New York; Lexington, Kentucky; Saratoga

Springs, New York; and Elmira, New York, I will be ever grateful for you and for the opportunity to serve the Lord with you. And to my current congregation, the Centenary United Methodist Church of Clemmons, North Carolina, thank you for embracing my leadership, your prayers, your commitment, and your service as we seek to make disciples for Christ for the transformation of the world.

A special thank you goes to my son, Vincent Jr., who was willing to work with me on this project and share his Master of Business Administration experience.

I thank Rev. Rebecca Irwin-Diehl, Lisa Blair, and Linda Triemstra-Cook at Judson Press for their editorial assistance and for their support in this project.

As I reflect on my journey in writing, I will ever be thankful for the seed planted by Rev. Dr. Henry H. Mitchell when I studied under him at the Ecumenical Center for Black Church Studies in Los Angeles, California.

Last but most importantly, I thank Jesus Christ, my Savior, who is my inspiration. May this work glorify and give praise to God, from whom all blessings flow.

—Vincent Wyatt Howell, DMin.

CHAPTER 1

An Overview of the MBA and Its Value to the Church

As we reflect on this idea of a pastor benefiting from the skills taught in an MBA program, we are captured by the words shared on the Harvard Business School's website: "Each day at HBS begins with one question: 'What will you do?' Because that's the truest way to prepare you for the larger question that matters most, here and in your career beyond our campus: 'What difference will you make in the world?'"[1] This is a profound question for leaders in business and in the church. The question raised is all about the leadership capacity of those in key roles in the organization. As such, it is our contention that church leaders must ask, "As a church leader, what difference will my leadership make in the church and the world?" With biblical and theological learning and MBA skills, pastors can be uniquely equipped for a new paradigm of leadership required in this modern culture.

An Overview of the MBA

All pastors are required to think out of the box as they lead congregations that are made up of diverse individuals—different age groups, races, genders, geographical areas, and worship preferences, just to name a few. Many times, creative thinking and managing diversity are skills that are not taught in a traditional Bible college or seminary. But they are taught in business schools or the MBA program.

So, let's start with understanding the context of MBA programs. The MBA program is designed to prepare students for leadership positions in a variety of organizations, for profit and not for profit. In the MBA program, students develop their understanding of complex organizations, strategies, and tactics and their execution. The main purpose of an MBA degree is to teach students how to manage an organization in every way or, in other words, to train qualified executives who have global visions for running their organizations.

The subject matter that is taught is quite varied, yet often the curriculum can be grouped into three main categories:

■ Analytical: accounting, business economics, researching operations, behavior in organizations, economic policy, statistics, and quantitative analysis
■ Functional: financial management, human resources management, marketing management, project management, and management of operations
■ Ethical: social and corporate responsibility, business ethics

While many programs provide opportunities for specialization, there is still an emphasis placed on broad knowledge since classes are structured to enrich analytical and decision-making skills through practical learning from problem definition, problem analysis, and problem solution. The MBA is typically a forty-eight-credit program focused on meeting the challenges of increasingly complex organizational environments. Programs are offered for full-time study, for part-time study with evening and online courses, and for executives.

Stacy Blackman, a writer for the *U.S. News and World Report*, has researched the MBA and highlights four benefits of this degree program.[2]

Business school gives new skills or strengthens skills and knowledge that will benefit career growth. While many MBA students go into such areas as finance or consulting, "the hard and soft skills acquired during an MBA program are transferable to myriad other roles."[3] Today, if we look at where a number of MBAs are working, we will see them serving in childcare, technology, healthcare, consumer goods, government, the military, nonprofits, and many other organizations. The career growth skills that can be strengthened during MBA studies include intellectual creativity, leadership, critical thinking, analysis, cross-cultural awareness, communication, and information technology.

Having an MBA provides unique skills for addressing complex problems. Any leader with an MBA has a unique leadership-oriented skill set. The Graduate Management Admission Council highlighted in its 2016 poll about hiring that 96 percent of responding employers agreed that hiring business school graduates creates value for their organizations. The conclusion is that organizations "appreciate managers who have risen through the ranks, know the business inside and out and can get the job done. But they also like hiring MBAs for their ability to handle complex situations, be nimble and adapt in the face of a rapidly changing global environment."[4]

Most MBA programs offer specializations or concentrations that allow students to delve into the leadership subject matter. The degree courses provide students with an opportunity to sample different leadership components to see which best fits each person's leadership context. "Adding a concentration to an MBA is a good move for people who know exactly what they want to do with their career and who want to build a stronger skill base in that area."[5]

"At business school, [students] interact closely with talented individuals from all over the globe, which enhances the experience by exposing [them] to different business practices, cultures and points of view.[6] The connections one makes during the MBA promotes a network of colleagues that allows for knowledge sharing in the future. Ministry too is a connectional endeavor, and pastors having a network of colleagues for information sharing and camaraderie is of great value. Expanding that network with ministry and management colleagues can prove to be priceless.

The purpose of the MBA is to give students a wide knowledge to build business. An MBA is one of the most popular master's degree programs, with the highest demand in the world. The church may not be profit-oriented, but it does have customers, as businesses do, and organizational success.

Therefore, where do church leaders go from here? One consideration on leadership knowledge is the tendency to categorize: business leadership, manufacturing leadership, church leadership, or nonprofit organizational leadership, for example. With such affinity alignment, there is a possibility that leadership learning from one discipline is overlooked as a benefit for another discipline. Such is the case at times with church leadership. Many pastors complete their Master of Divinity degree and move into the top church leadership role (pastor) in a congregation. However, looking at the core of the MDiv curriculum—Bible, history, theology, preaching, pastoral care, field education, and thesis/project—there is limited leadership course work. Yet the role of the pastor includes these traditional roles, as well as management and leadership responsibilities. Furthermore, this management and leadership role of the pastor is critical as churches must face such questions as:

■ How do I manage human resources (organizational culture, planning for change, training and development, compensation, health and safety, recruitment, and retention)?

■ How do we develop and execute a strategic plan?

■ What management strategy is required as our congregation strives to reach the younger generation?

■ With a multi-campus church, how do we manage multiple facilities and the associated assets?

■ What is the best way to manage not only the multiple projects we execute but also the portfolio of projects required to execute the five-year strategic plan of the church? These topics, and more, are ones that pastors address as part of the role of pastor and chief executive of a congregation. A pastor combining MDiv and MBA knowledge provides a foundation for emphasizing the importance of church leadership along with bringing the best management and leadership practices to the faith community context. The Boston College School of Theology and Ministry, which offers a joint MA/MBA degree, emphasizes the importance of church leadership stating that one of its objectives "is to prepare practitioners who have a commitment to work with the church in bringing best management practices to the church and related agencies, while bringing theological expertise and a social-ethical perspective to management in these contexts."[7]

The Value of the MBA to the Church

Tech companies are organizations. Government departments are organizations. Consulting firms are organizations. And, like these entities, the church is an organization. The common thread of each of these organizations is people. Leadership experts will highlight that people have always been essential to any organization, large or small. The essence of this conclusion is that people provide inspiration, creativity, skills, and motivation that keep an organization alive. They also provide the competencies necessary to make an organization function. In the context of the church, the people in the church often bring skills related to teaching, leadership, work, accounting, or speaking. And unquestionably, they provide the labor that produces ministries that the church organization supplies. They are a major and the most important resource that an organization—sacred or secular—has.

In order for the organization to be effective, capable leaders are required. This is especially true in the church leadership context. What is capable leadership in the church? In a study to provide a training tool to help congregations, pastors, and other church leaders to work effectively together to accomplish God's mission, the Christian Reformed Church in North America provides a definition: "Effective Christian leadership is the process of helping a group embody in its corporate life the practices that shape vital Christian life, community, and witness in ways that are faithful to Jesus Christ and the gospel and appropriate to the particular group's setting, resources, and purpose."[8]

A critical foundation of leadership is leadership development. Leadership is not effective simply because a pastor has been called or appointed to a congregation. Leadership capability must be built. When pastors purposely pursue leadership and management training focused on church management, they build a toolbox filled with leadership techniques and tools to navigate the increasingly complex realities of church work. This also puts the pastor in a position to help further develop church lay leaders. As is pointed out by Charles Zech, professor of economics and director of the Master of Science in Church Management program at Villanova University, "The church is not a business, but it does have a responsibility to be a good steward of its resources." The Church Management program hopes to "develop church leaders of the future, grounded in theology and possessing the tools necessary to strengthen the church in a changing world."[9] Being a good steward of church resources includes leadership capacity development.

Over the past few years, there has been a growth in the number of universities that offer the MBA or similar degrees for pastors. It is helpful to understand why universities and seminaries have collaborated to offer this opportunity to pastors as we look at why MBA skills are of value to the church.

Howard University, located in Washington, DC, states that its MDiv/MBA degree program "is tailored to meet the needs of today's leaders who wish to gain a strong theological education and management education to enhance their effectiveness in ministry, business, non-profit, and public sector careers."[10]

Seattle Pacific University, founded by Free Methodist pioneers in 1891, speaks about the integration of business and theology:

> The scandals rocking the business world in the last decade have left younger generations with increased levels of cynicism. From Enron to Wall Street, stories of greed and selfishness permeate our cultural consciousness. With business schools teaching profit maximization as the sole purpose of business, the academy has done little to alter society's pre-conceived notions of the marketplace.
>
> Unfortunately, the church speaks minimally to those in the business world. Aside from pithy statements suggesting how the Christian businessperson must strive to live morally in the business place, the church views business in purely instrumental terms. Put differently, the predominant view of business in the church is that it exists to bankroll ministry.
>
> But what if business holds intrinsic value in the Kingdom of God? What if Christians could find vocation in the marketplace? Grounded in sound theological reflection and rigorous business education, Seattle Pacific University's School of Theology and School of Business and Economics provide dual degrees in business and theology.
>
> This program combining an MBA with an MA in Business and Applied Theology or an MDiv focuses on rethinking the way business does business.[11]

A third university that highlights the value of MBA skills for the church is Palm Beach Atlantic University (PBA), which highlights the value of MBA skills to the church by stating that "being on the leadership team of many churches today requires both theological education and business acumen. Ministers must understand how the church fits into the broader community and how to address complex business challenges."[12]

This short review shows clearly that there are seminaries that highlight the importance of leadership, management, and business acumen for pastors and church leaders. Additionally, a pastor who has earned the MDiv and is currently completing an MBA shares his perspective. John Roland, who also has pastored three churches, highlights the following five reasons why pastors should pursue an MBA.

> 1. [An] MBA is a more functional degree in leading a church than a DMin—With budgets, buildings, capital campaigns, church plants, [and] marketing of the church, [the] MBA will be far more practical than taking additional theology courses.
>
> 2. [An] MBA is respected and translates better to the congregation—Congregational members will better understand their pastor's skill set if he adds an MBA [rather] than just additional theological graduate hours in pursuing a DMin. [The MBA] allows the pastor to better navigate the dangerous "waters" of running a nonprofit organization. We are called as Christians to be "Innocent as doves, wise as serpents."
>
> 3. Education from an MBA will allow [pastors] to become more strategic in the organizational structure of a church—[L]earning people is vital in leading a church. Obviously following God's leading in all things we are to use our brains in strategizing outreach, becoming entrepreneurial in planting churches, and intentional in our missions.
>
> 4. [An] MBA diversifies one's education— Understanding the business side of running an organization is a blind spot for many pastors with a solely theological degree background.

5. [An] MBA provides an education which can translate well bivocationally.[13]

In summary, the MBA degree can offer pastors the chance to develop a wide range of general business and organizational knowledge to supplement their theological training. This becomes a benefit to the pastor and local church laity as they partner in ministry strategically to understand how the local church fits into the broader community and how to address complex challenges facing the church and the community it serves.

Notes

1. "The HBS Difference—What Will You Do?," Harvard Business School, https://www.hbs.edu/mba/the-hbs-difference/Pages/default.aspx.

2. Stacy Blackman, "4 Key Career Benefits from MBA Programs," US News & World Report, April 8, 2016, https://www.usnews.com/education/blogs/mba-admissions-strictly-business/2016/04/08/4-key-career-benefits-from-mba-programs. *U.S. News & World Report* ranks and rates graduate and undergraduate programs.

3. Ibid.

4. Ibid. The Graduate Management Council is an international organization that is the leading source of research and information about quality graduate management education. It also provides a tool that is considered the most reliable predictor of academic success in graduate business studies.

5. Ibid.

6. Ibid.

7. Boston College School of Theology & Ministry, bc.edu/content/bc-web/schools/stm/academics/program-pages/master-of-arts-theology-ministry.html#dual.

8. Ivery White, *Effective Leadership in the Church* (Raleigh, NC: Lulu Press Inc., 2019), 19.

9. "Management Skills for More Effective Ministry," Church Executive, February 1, 2017, https://churchexecutive.com/archives /lifetime-learning.

10. "Master of Divinity/Master of Business Administration," Howard University School of Divinity, last modified June 27, 2019, http://divinity.howard.edu/academics_master_business_admin.html.

11. "MBA/MA in Business and Applied Theology or MBA/ MDiv," Seattle Pacific University, https://spu.edu/academics /seattle-pacific-seminary/programs/dual-degrees/theology-and-business.

12. "Master of Divinity/ Master of Business Administration," Palm Beach Atlantic University, https://learn-well.pba.edu/academics /som-grad/mdiv-mba.html.

13. John Roland, "Why Pastors Should Pursue an MBA Instead of DMin," SBC Voices, August 12, 2014, http://sbcvoices.com/ why-pastors-should-pursue-an-mba-instead-of-dmin/.

CHAPTER 2

A Theological Foundation for Pastors' Use of MBA Skills

Back in 2017, while serving a church in the New York State area, I (Vincent) was asked to serve on a committee called the Conference Leadership Team. In the discussion about roles and responsibilities associated with this new responsibility, a key component was to assist with developing leadership capacity. For me, defining these two words was my starting point.

The word *leadership* means many things to different people. But the one definition that I feel best fits was captured by Lolly Daskal, president and CEO of Lead from Within, a global consultancy that specializes in leadership and entrepreneurial development. Lolly quoted Miles Munroe:[1] "Leadership is the capacity to influence others through inspiration motivated by passion, generated by vision, produced by a conviction, ignited by a purpose."[2] When I think about the word *capacity* in light of leadership, I think about the ability to exercise the maximum potential. In other words, my role on the conference leadership team was to help develop and execute strategies so that leaders in the church could lead local churches in reaching their maximum potential for the kingdom of God.

Leading a congregation to achieve more than it thinks it can; leading a congregation in achieving more than it currently is achieving; leading a congregation to achieve its maximum ability or giving our best in serving the Lord—those are awesome responsibilities. These are the pastor's roles. And that is what the Lord requires of those whom he has called, as we are taught in Ephesians 4:4-6. The point is this: pastors are to lead. And church leadership is primarily by influence. Hebrews 13:7 (NIV) says, "Remember your leaders, who spoke the word of God to you. Consider the outcome of their way of life and imitate their faith." This means that our leadership ability, skill, and capacity are critical in how we serve and influence others in Christian development. As the Word of God teaches, we are to lead with a Christ-like example.

How can pastors develop leadership capacity? By all means, our foundation is the Word of God. Many pastors pursue some level of postsecondary education. But is it enough to get a Bible college degree and stop there? Is it enough to get a Master of Divinity or Master of Ministry degree and stop there? Is it enough to earn a Doctor of Ministry and stop there? Greg Smith, who spent more than fifteen years serving congregations in lay and pastoral roles, shares an insightful perspective:

> While most Protestant denominations either require or strongly recommend those preparing for ministry as pastor earn a seminary degree (normally the Master of Divinity) few groups have established protocols requiring that academic preparation include significant training in business or organizational leadership. Since most congregations are small in size (approximately two-thirds have fewer than 200 members), pastors are often tasked with the daily oversight of the daily operations of the church as a business. In this environment, clergy are expected to competently handle the congregation's facilities and finances.[3]

As a bi-vocational pastor, I benefited from serving in leadership roles in the private sector prior to entering seminary and from a variety of leadership and management courses during my lifelong learning studies. These have included business school experience (I earned a master's degree in management). Furthermore, I have taught business ethics at the graduate-school level. By serving small and medium-sized congregations, as well as various denomination-al district- and conference-level committees, and by volunteering with nonprofit organizations, my ministry has benefitted a great deal regarding leadership and church management and administra-tion matters.

A key consideration for pastors thinking about expanding their organizational leadership and management knowledge via MBA-type course work is whether there is a theological foundation for complementing biblical studies with expanded MBA learning. For us as pastors, Jesus should be at the center of our lives and ministry, meaning that we should consider him in everything we do. So, as we look at the theological foundation for this type of leadership education, I propose three Scriptures as a start.

The Book of Proverbs

First, from the book of wisdom, God says to us, "How much bet-ter to get wisdom than gold, to get insight rather than silver!" (Proverbs 16:16, NIV). God directs his followers, lay and pastoral, to get wisdom. A biblical definition of wisdom, provided by Jack Wellman, pastor of the Mulvane Brethren Church in Mulvane, Kansas, writes:

> Wisdom isn't simply intelligence or knowledge or even understanding. It is the ability to use these to think and act in such a way that common sense prevails and choices are beneficial and productive... Wisdom begins with rever-ence for God and a fear for Him and His Word. That's where wisdom begins. Where there is no fear of the Lord, there can never be any true wisdom. It's just not possible.[4]

As pastors in the church, our reverence (fear) of the Lord should drive us toward a life of ever-increasing learning and knowledge from life experience, so that our wisdom can increase in support of ministry service and leadership.

The Letters to Timothy

A second passage for our theological foundation comes from 2 Timothy 2:15: "Study to shew thyself approved unto God, a workman that needeth not to be ashamed, rightly dividing the word of truth" (KJV). A key word in this translation of the verse for pastoral leaders is "study." The word *study*, as defined by Webster's dictionary, means "application of the mental faculties to the acquisition of knowledge." Looking at other translations of this verse also provides enlightenment:

> "Do your best to present yourself to God as one approved, a worker who does not need to be ashamed and who correctly handles the word of truth" (NIV).
>
> "Work hard so God can say to you, 'Well done.' Be a good workman, one who does not need to be ashamed when God examines your work. Know what his Word says and means" (TLB).
>
> "Be diligent to present yourself approved to God as a workman who does not need to be ashamed, accurately handling the word of truth" (NASB).

In studying this verse in various translations, we learn that part of our role as pastoral leaders includes not only studying but also doing our best, working hard, and being diligent as we lead. It also suggests that we maintain leadership knowledge for ministry in an ever-changing world. This principle applies to all aspects of ministry: discipleship development, ministry development, and organizational development. It is important that we be diligent in applying all our energy to the service of God, including continuing leadership education that will allow us to stand before God, as Paul cautioned Timothy, knowing that we have been diligent. Nothing will help us more to please God than to handle carefully and correctly God's written Word. We should look to the written Word of God with the same reverence as the psalmist who wrote, "Thy word is a lamp unto my feet, and a light unto my path" (Psalm 119:105, KJV).

Second Timothy 2:15 is such an important verse in Scripture that every pastor needs to pay great attention to it. Everything we do to lead the congregation, to develop new ministries, and to enhance our personal ministry by continuing education requires that we take quality time to study and research new tools and knowledge when it comes to the service of the Lord and the people of God.

The Book of Nehemiah

A third applicable Scripture is the Old Testament book of Nehemiah. In my book about church project management,[5] I make the case that Nehemiah's rebuilding of the wall is a good example of how God uses him to lead a project. A key component of a successful project is leadership. In dissecting the book of Nehemiah, pastors and lay leaders can garner a number of leadership lessons. As Michelle L. Rayburn's Bible study highlights, writes, "The book of Nehemiah shows church leaders how to tackle difficult leadership assignments that God assigns us. Here are some highlights:"[6]

■ Prepare for the mission: A leader must have passion (Nehemiah 1–2).

■ Share and sustain the vision: A leader must be able to bring others on board (Nehemiah 3–5).

■ Manage the opposition: A leader must learn how to handle conflict (Nehemiah 3:3-5; 4:1-11; 6:1-16).

■ Celebrate and continue the completed mission: Don't forget to thank God and to keep the mission pure (Nehemiah 12:27, 40, 43; 13:1-31).

These competencies are core leadership skills. These skills, based on the book of Nehemiah, have been shown to help God's leaders. The study of MBA competencies by pastoral leaders allows pastors to gain a well-documented benefit of earning an MBA: leadership development. And because pastors in the local church must lead by example and must lead the congregation in faith formation and leadership development, attaining MBA competencies also puts the pastor in a position to be better able to teach those same skills to those in the congregation for long-term development of leadership capacity.

Notes

1. Miles Munroe was an evangelist, author, speaker, and leadership consultant who founded and led the Bahamas Faith Ministries International.

2. Lolly Daskal, "100 Answers to the Question: What Is Leadership?," Inc., March 28, 2016, https://www.inc.com/lolly-daskal/100-answers-to-the-question-what-is-leadership.html.

3. Smith currently serves as director of social enterprise at the Mansfield Mission Center and as adjunct professor of religion at Hodges University, https://sowhatfaith.com/2012/11/28/pastoral-mba/.

4. Jack Wellman, "What Is the Bible Definition of Wisdom? How Are We Wise in God's Eyes?," Christian Crier, May 22, 2015, http://www.patheos.com/blogs/christiancrier/2015/05/22/what-is-the-bible-definition-of-wisdom-how-are-we-wise-in-gods-eyes. Wellman is also senior writer at What Christians Want to Know, whose mission is to equip, encourage, and energize Christians.

5. Vincent Wyatt Howell, *Managing Projects in Ministry* (Valley Forge, PA: Judson Press, 2017).

6. Michelle L. Rayburn, "Nehemiah: Learning Leadership," July 13, 2009, https://www.christianitytoday.com/biblestudies/n/nehemiah-learning-leadership-4-session-study.html.

CHAPTER 3

Principles of Decision-Making

Within the church, some decisions are based on democratic vote. Some decisions are made by the most vocal contingent. Other times decisions are made by the pastor. Sometimes the results are positive, but some decisions are bad decisions. They can cause hard feelings or harm team or committee morale when making autocratic decisions without involving others.

So, the idea of effective decision-making is critically important. Scripture advises:

> I will instruct you and teach you in the way you should go;
> I will guide you with My eye.
> Do not be like the horse or like the mule,
> Which have no understanding,
> Which must be harnessed with bit and bridle,
> Else they will not come near you.
> —Psalm 32:8-9 (NKJV)

In decision-making, we must discern God's will. Personally, I (Vincent) hear the psalmist advising that church leaders are to depend on God's leading, not our gut feeling or our committee consensus. As pastors, this is a continuing responsibility as we lead daily throughout our pastoral lives. The opposite of following God's leading in decision-making is to rely on self-assurance, which ultimately threatens or interferes with our ministry. Following God's leadership as we look to apply tools that help us make decisions based on our Spirit-led leadership capacity means we are open to and are conscious of the fact that God is guiding our future and wants to share God's vision with us.

All kinds of decisions need to be made in the church. Some are small, and some are critical—things like capital campaigns, capital procurement, purchasing real estate, starting a new ministry, hiring critical staff personnel, just to name a few. These are decisions that at times affect church strategy, require significant investment, and have long-term effects on church organizational effectiveness and mission accomplishment. As such, a question should be raised: What is the best way to make important decisions? Is it a matter of committees meeting and voting their conscience? Is "majority rules" the best option? The role of the pastor of a congregation requires the ability to make good decisions. Wrong decision-making processes can affect the entire church. It is crucial for church leaders to understand the weight behind each decision they make. Therefore, it is important for pastors to continually improve their decision-making skills.

When major decisions are at stake, many leaders can feel paralyzed by the magnitude and complexity of the decisions. Sometimes all of us, including pastors, can project false confidence and take decisive but uninformed action. Fortunately, a solution exists to help pastoral leaders make or lead their congregation in making good decisions. In many MBA programs, there is a course that focuses on decision analysis and decision-making.

In this chapter, our focus is how the pastoral leader can make important and complex decisions, analyze risks, and map out clear plans of action. You will learn methods to map out risks, rewards, and varying outcomes so you can logically assess the consequences of your decisions and make more confident and strategic decisions.

What Is Decision Analysis?

Decision-making, even in the church, is not trivial. Our goal as leaders is to make wiser and more valuable decisions in every circumstance. To do this requires the ability to break down the elements of decision-making and use tools, models, and forecasting tools to reduce uncertainty in important decisions situations. At the same time, considerations need to be made regarding use of data, quantitative analysis, community and congregational insight, and psychological or rational influences that affect both individual and team decisions. Furthermore, decision-making requires that we learn ways to circumvent personal biases that can negatively influence the decision, as well as organizational effectiveness. By so doing, both the leader and those involved in the decision process are able to evolve their awareness of which elements truly matter to the achievement of church objectives and mission and shift from intuitive to data-driven thinking.

With this as our foundation, we will provide an MBA-oriented definition of decision analysis:

> The term decision analysis was coined in 1964 by Ronald A. Howard, professor of management science and engineering at Stanford University. Decision analysis refers to a systematic, quantitative, and interactive approach to addressing and evaluating important choices confronted by organisations in the private and public sector. Decision analysis is interdisciplinary and draws on theories from the fields of psychology, economics, and management science. It utilises a variety of tools which include models for decision-making under conditions of uncertainty or multiple objectives; techniques of risk analysis and risk assessment; experimental and descriptive studies of decision-making behaviour; economic analysis of competitive and strategic decisions; techniques for facilitating decision-making by groups; and computer modeling software and expert systems for decision support.[1]

Why is this important for the church? In looking at this definition, we see an important concept that is highlighted is data and the use of data in decision-making. There are key value propositions for churches using data in decision-making. Meredith Morris, a church consultant for ACS Technologies, which develops technology solutions specifically for faith-based organizations, including churches that are listed in the 100 Fastest Growing Churches in America, points out:

> **Numbers matter.** Numbers represent people. Someone counted the thousands of people Jesus fed with five loaves and two fish, and someone counted the leftover baskets because the numbers told the story of Jesus' love and power. Others counted the 3,000 people who came to faith following Peter's Pentecost sermon because it mattered.
>
> **People's needs matter.** The Apostle Paul had his finger on the pulse of the churches he planted. He wrote letters to them that dealt with specific issues they faced. Paul knew their needs, kept up with their growth and their struggles because he listened to couriers who traveled long distances with important messages. He used this information to pray for them and speak words of life to them.
>
> **Churches that effectively gather and analyze data make better decisions for people.** Good decisions come from good information. Churches that know their people adjust their processes to fit their people rather than trying to fit people into their rigid processes.[2]

Decision Data

To help with decisions, data is a requirement. At a basic level, a starting point for church data collection begins with three key areas. By attending to the three areas, the church and its leaders will be able to look at data and determine the questions that need to be asked. For example, what does someone's giving pattern tell us about their commitment to the church? Is commitment changing? Who is coming back to the church and who is not? Which types of communication help us to be most effective? Below are some additional examples of data that can help with decision-making:

■ Basic details: number of people in your congregation, their age, marital status, and address

■ Giving trends by age or term: this helps provide insights into your church's effectiveness in promoting contributions across age ranges and seasonal patterns.

■ Member participation and interests: this helps with gaining insight into what programs and ministries are popular and what kind of person is attending them. If people aren't getting involved, you need to determine why not (and then work toward resolution). Knowing past involvement and interests should benefit in building a profile for the kind of ministry events the church should be offering.

Many times data collected is limited to the number of attendees or weekly offering. Yet, often, other data is available but not collected. For example, even if a church has a visitor information card that they ask newcomers to complete, is this information put into a database so that it can be analyzed and used for ministry development? Consider these possibilities for ministry data:

■ Number of visitors each month
■ Average number of visitors each week
■ Number of visitors who are millennials versus those over 60 years of age
■ Number of visitors who are unchurched
■ Number of repeat visitors
■ Diversity of visitors: number of visitors who are of a different ethnicity each week, month, and year
■ Number of visitors attending special programs

The question then becomes, what data can we collect that will prove beneficial to helping the church achieve its mission and objectives? There is a plethora of data available to churches; the key is how the data is used. A *Washington Monthly* article, "Christian America Is in Decline—Here's Why It Impacts Everyone," concludes that even in this time when we are bombarded with media stories about church decline, some churches are flourishing because they discover new ways to minister and meet Christian formation and community needs.[3] Matt Engel of the Colorado-based technology firm Gloo advises that "one of the newest ways churches can determine these needs is with [big] data."[4] Big data, though there are many definitions, is defined in a *Forbes* article as "'the ability of society to harness information in novel ways to produce useful insights or goods and services of significant value' and 'things one can do at a large scale that cannot be done at a smaller one, to extract new insights or create new forms of value.'"[5]

There are many ways and resources to collect data to understand the needs of the community around your congregation for decision-making. Engel suggest a few tools that pastoral leaders and congregations can benefit from:

■ Use analytics from social media to know more about your following. "There are many ways to collect and analyze data from social media. Facebook has Insights, and Twitter has Analytics. Additional tools are available through LinkedIn, Instagram, and other social media channels."[6]

■ Surveys and assessments give you first-party information about your people. "Many churches use surveys to assess the needs of their members through first-party information. These can be done through software like SurveyMonkey or SurveyGizmo to assess the spiritual and temporal needs of your congregants. Some churches find it helpful to collect data through formal assessments, but data can also be collected in meetings, private interviews, or detailed reports from church leaders."[7]

■ Demographic reports tell you information about ages, income, and more. "Demographics can provide a lot of insight into your community. Through these reports, you can often access religious affiliation, marital status, household income, and the ages of residents."[8]

■ Third-party data vendors create models that predict people's behavior. "While some data can be collected from individual sources, there are services that gather, sort, and provide data for their clients on a much larger scale—searching millions in their databases and producing thousands of data points per person for analysis. This information creates predictive models of behavior.[9]

Decision-Making and Decision Processes

Before we look at tools that can help churches make effective decisions, let's first look at the types of decisions most leaders and organizations are involved with. Researching this topic from a number of sources results in several ways to classify decisions, of which we will emphasize six and describe each from the perspective of the church and church leaders: programmed and non-programmed; strategic; tactical; organizational; major and minor; and group.

Programmed decisions are based on the idea that these decisions are routine and repetitive. These decisions may be related to the ongoing functions of the organization and typically are governed by the organization's standard operating procedures and policies. For example, the church secretary may run out of copier paper, but the church has a standing account for ordering supplies. The secretary makes a programmed decision to replace supplies instead of elevating the decision. A non-programmed decision is a decision that is more complex and requires broader decision-maker involvement. For example, non-programmed decisions could be related to a community organization requesting use of the church facility. Though there may be procedures for renting the building, likely a number of people will be consulted to verify there are no programs planned that aren't on the schedule, whether there is maintenance planned by trustees, or whether the requesting organization's mission is in conflict with the church mission. These decisions are usually made at a higher level since each decision of this type is unique.

Strategic decisions are those that involve or impact organizational objectives, goals, and other important policy matters. These decisions usually involve capital expenditures and impact church budgets. Strategic decisions are not repetitive (meaning they don't occur on a regular basis) and therefore require careful analysis and evaluation of many alternatives. A church deciding on the location of a second campus is a decision that is taken at the higher level of leadership in a church.

By contrast, decisions pertaining to various courses of action within the church organization are tactical or policy decisions. These involve pastoral and church administrative leaders as they have long-term impacts on church functioning. For example, decisions regarding facilities, number and type of services, and communication channels are tactical decisions.

Organizational decision can be of two types in the church. Fundamentally, organizational decisions are those which the chief executive of the church (pastor) makes in her or his official capacity. These may also be decisions that the pastor chooses to delegate to others. If a church is trying to decide whether to affiliate with a particular convention (e.g., American Baptist Convention or National Baptist Convention), that too would be an organizational decision.

As you likely have noticed from the decision types discussed above, there are major and minor decisions that need to be made. Decisions pertaining to building a new multipurpose center is a major decision. In the church, major decisions such as this often involve the church leadership team and the congregation. Purchasing of office supplies and printer ink is a minor decision which can be made by the church office administrator.

The last decision classification is group decisions. Whether a church is large or small, it often has committees. Committees typically make group decisions (sometimes referred to as collective decision-making). This is particularly true when the church operates using shared lay and pastoral leadership. Group decision-making is a formal process by which several committee team leaders work together to make a decision or the ministry team itself is tasked with decision-making. In a collective decision-making context, the group can use different methods to arrive at decisions, such as voting, consensus, and electing a leader to make the final decision. Many leadership experts advise that group decision-making take more time as the team works toward making sure all team members are participating and that there is mutual understanding and consensus. Nonetheless, this is an important decision-making process, especially for small and medium-size churches. Gregory Hamel, writing in "The Advantages and Disadvantages of Group Decision-Making," provides the following encouragement when using group decision-making (the quote has been adapted for a church leadership context):

> If [church ministry team leaders] have fundamental disagreements about how to approach a decision, it may be difficult—if not impossible—for a group to reach a consensus, which is a result that everyone can agree to even if it represents the lowest common denominator of all ideas offered. The desire for consensus also can cause decision makers to avoid conflict and the [presentation] of alternatives. The tendency to conform to the group and avoid raising potentially unpopular ideas is called groupthink. Groupthink can reduce knowledge sharing and creativity, thereby diminishing some of the key benefits of group decision making. When you understand the advantages and disadvantages of group decision making, you can more easily choose a course of action that's best for your [church and the people it serves], which ultimately is the top priority.[10]

In the next chapter, we'll give a model for decision-making, so that readers will have a clear view of how they can use the principles of decision-making.

Notes

1. "Definition of decision analysis," Financial Times, http://markets.ft.com/research/lexicon/term?term=decision-analysis.

2. Meredith Morris, "What Role Does Data Have in the Church?," ASC Technologies, January 27, 2017, https://ministry.acst.com/role-data-church/.

3. Anthony B. Pinn, and Tom Krattenmaker, "Christian America Is in Decline—Here's Why It Impacts Everyone," Washington Monthly, December 23, 2016, https://washingtonmonthly.com/2016/12/23/-christian-america-is-in-decline-heres-why-it-impacts-everyone/.

4. Matt Engel, "Use Big Data to Engage Your People and Grow Your Church," Gloo, April 19, 2019, https://blog.gloo.us/big-data-for-churches-introduction.

5. Gil Press, "12 Big Data Definitions: What's Yours?," *Forbes* online, September 3, 2014, https://www.forbes.com/sites/gilpress/2014/09/03/12-big-data-definitions-whats-yours/. The article quotes Viktor Mayer-Schönberger and Kenneth Cukier, *Big Data: A Revolution That Will Transform How We Live, Work, and Think* (London: John Murray, 2013).

6. Engel, "Use Big Data."

7. Ibid.

8. Ibid.

9. Ibid.

10. Gregory Hamel, "The Advantages & Disadvantages of Group Decision-Making," Bizfluent, October 18, 2018, https://bizfluent.com/info-8212675-advantages-disadvantages-group-decisionmaking.html.

CHAPTER 4

Models for Decision-Making

In this chapter, we will present two decision-making models from which churches can benefit. As was noted in chapter three, many small- to medium-sized churches need to make decisions using groups such as administrative council and various boards, committees, and auxiliaries.

The Nominal Group Technique

The first model we will present is the Nominal Group Technique (NGT). The NGT is defined by the American Society for Quality as "a structured method for group brainstorming that encourages contributions from everyone." The University of Vermont's Center for Rural Studies provides an overview for how churches can use this tool.[1]

Preparation:

■ The audience will be seated in groups of no more than 12 persons around a table. Two people will serve as group leaders, sharing the responsibilities, one working as a facilitator, one as a recorder. The group leader/facilitator will ask each participant to introduce him/herself in a sentence or two. The group leader/facilitator will review the procedure for Nominal Group Technique. The nominal group is a structured group that meets to gather information about a specific concern; that is, to identify problems and priorities. Individuals work alone but in a group setting.

■ Research in group dynamics indicates that more ideas are expressed by individuals working alone but in a group environment than by individuals engaged in a formal group discussion. The Nominal Group Technique is a good way of getting many ideas from a group. It has advantages over the usual committee approach to identifying ideas. Group consensus can be reached faster and everyone has equal opportunity to present their ideas.

There are five steps in the Nominal Group Technique:

1. Individuals silently write down their ideas in a few words.

2. Each group member presents, but does not discuss, one of the ideas on his or her list. The ideas are recorded on newsprint. The leader then asks each person for a second idea, and so on, until all ideas are recorded. All ideas are recorded as presented.

3. The leader reads each idea on the newsprint and asks if there are questions, interpretations, or explanations. It's a good idea at this point to number the ideas.

4. The leader asks each person to write down, in a few minutes, the ideas that seem especially important. Some people may feel only a few items are important; others may feel all items are important. The leader then goes down the list and records the number of people who consider each item a priority.

5. Finally, participants rate each item from no importance (0) to top priority (10). A person may have several top priority items (all 10s), or only one top priority. The leader then collects and calculates the ratings and records the cumulative rating for each item. Starting with the issue receiving the highest priority, you may search for solutions to the issue using the same method. Action steps may then be identified and prioritized.

Figure 4.1. A Flow Chart for Applying the Nominal Group Technique

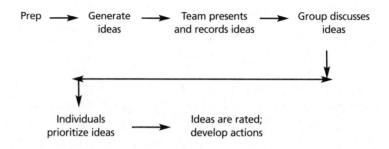

Kepner-Tregoe (K-T) Problem-Solving

The second model is a more structured approach to decision-making. It can be used in a group or individual context. For pastors, this role of decision-making is an important one, as it affects the action and work that need to take place once the decision is made. But there are also human relationship implications. Therefore, when decisions need to be made at the pastoral or auxiliary/committee level, how decisions are made should not be taken lightly. There are a number of ways decisions can be made: unilaterally, unilaterally with input, majority rule, delegation, or ministry team consensus. Each of these models has advantages and disadvantages whereby, once the decision is made, someone may not be happy.

Again, it is important that we remember that, even with decisions, our guidance should be founded on Scripture. In regard to church decision-making, we must always be focused on determining God's will, trusting God to lead when difficult decisions need to be made, and seeking wisdom through the Bible.

God counsels us in this regard through the Word. Writing to the Ephesians, the apostle Paul reminds us, "In him we were also chosen, having been predestined according to the plan of him who works out everything in conformity with the purpose of his will"

(Ephesians 1:11, NIV). In the book of wisdom we are directed to seek God's guidance: "Where there is no guidance, a people falls, but in an abundance of counselors there is safety" (Proverbs 11:14, ESV). And even in decision-making, we are to "pray without ceasing" (1 Thessalonians 5:17, KJV).

So, with God's Word and God's leading as our foundation, in this final section I want to take us beyond the kind of decisions we make to a process of decision-making. As a bi-vocational pastor, I have had success using a decision-making process called the Kepner Tregoe (KT) method, which was developed by Charles Kepner and Benjamin Tregoe. Kepner and Tregoe went on to found Kepner-Tregoe, Inc., a sixty-year-old global management consulting firm which provides a unique combination of training and consulting services designed specifically to get to the root cause of problems and permanently address organizational challenges. The KT systematic, data-driven approach to problem-solving concentrates on delivering measurable results to any organization looking to improve quality and effectiveness while reducing overall costs.

What I like about this process or methodology, if you will, is that it provides a means for people to make decisions with data and human insight. After all, data and software don't make decisions or solve problems, people do. So the human element is still relevant. The Kepner Tregoe methodology is described as follows:

> Problems occur in any given organization. Often there is pressure of time to solve the problems and it is debatable what the right way of solving these problems is. The Kepner Tregoe method (KT-method) is a problem analysis model in which the "problem" is disconnected from the "decision." An English synonym for this problem solving method is Problem Solving and Decision Making (PSDM).[2]

Let's now look at how this methodology can be used. First, there are four components of the KT process that Kepner and Tregoe describe in *The New Rational Manager:*[3]

■ Problem analysis (PA): the objective is to define the problem and determine its root cause

■ Decision analysis (DA): the objective is making a good choice or decision, with particular focus on identifying alternatives and performing a risk analysis for each, so that the best choice can be made

■ Potential problem analysis (PPA): the objective is to make sure there is consideration for future events and any associated consequences for decisions that have been made. In PPA, the organization is doing additional examination of the alternatives (for example, from the DA conducted above) to determine potential problems and negative consequences. With this information, the organization can develop proposed actions (and triggers that will initiate action) in order minimize the risk in the case where the potential problems identified come to bear.

■ Situation appraisal (SA): the SA is used to clarify a current or pending situation, summarize concerns, and choose a plan of action. Kepner and Tregoe describe it as follows:[4]

> Situation Appraisal, by contrast, consists of analytical techniques. This process builds the framework for daily use of rational-process idea. It enables managers to make best possible use of the techniques of Problem Analysis, Decision Analysis, and Potential Problem Analysis by showing them:
>
> Where to begin
> How to recognize situations that require action
> How to break apart overlapping and confusing lessons

How to set priorities

How to manage a number of simultaneous activities efficiently

Figure 4.2 provides a graphical representation of the three key processes, with Situation Appraisal as the point of intersection. Each process has five steps, with key questions that need to be asked and data or information that the decision-making team needs to gather and review. A number of online resources can coach you through these processes (see the resource section), but the following example will allow you to see the Decision Analysis segment.

Figure 4.2. The Kepner Tregoe Model

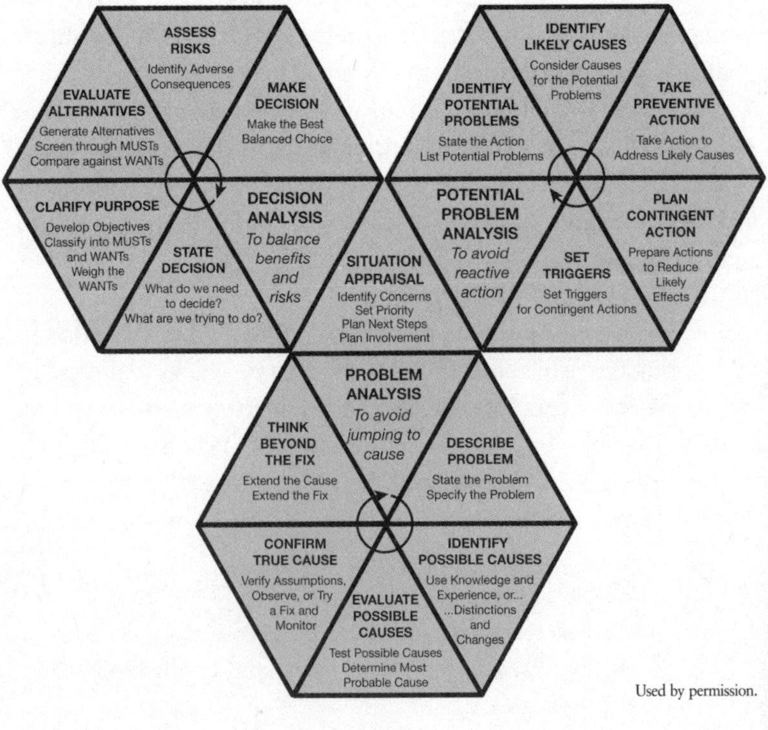

ASSESS RISKS
Identify Adverse Consequences

MAKE DECISION
Make the Best Balanced Choice

EVALUATE ALTERNATIVES
Generate Alternatives
Screen through MUSTs
Compare against WANTs

CLARIFY PURPOSE
Develop Objectives
Classify into MUSTs and WANTs
Weigh the WANTs

STATE DECISION
What do we need to decide?
What are we trying to do?

DECISION ANALYSIS
To balance benefits and risks

SITUATION APPRAISAL
Identify Concerns
Set Priority
Plan Next Steps
Plan Involvement

IDENTIFY LIKELY CAUSES
Consider Causes for the Potential Problems

IDENTIFY POTENTIAL PROBLEMS
State the Action
List Potential Problems

TAKE PREVENTIVE ACTION
Take Action to Address Likely Causes

POTENTIAL PROBLEM ANALYSIS
To avoid reactive action

SET TRIGGERS
Set Triggers for Contingent Actions

PLAN CONTINGENT ACTION
Prepare Actions to Reduce Likely Effects

PROBLEM ANALYSIS
To avoid jumping to cause

THINK BEYOND THE FIX
Extend the Cause
Extend the Fix

DESCRIBE PROBLEM
State the Problem
Specify the Problem

CONFIRM TRUE CAUSE
Verify Assumptions,
Observe, or Try a Fix and Monitor

EVALUATE POSSIBLE CAUSES
Test Possible Causes
Determine Most Probable Cause

IDENTIFY POSSIBLE CAUSES
Use Knowledge and Experience, or...
...Distinctions and Changes

Used by permission.

An Example of the Kepner Tregoe Analysis

In this example, we want to look at the KT process and use an example based on the Decision Analysis (DA) in order to get to a decision alternative. What you will be doing is summarized in the five steps below.

1. Write a succinct decision statement about what the team wants to decide. Use the first four problem-solving steps to gather information.

2. Specify objectives of the decision and divide into must-haves and wants.

3. Evaluate each option against the must-haves. Decide if the alternative is a go versus no-go item. For example, if you want to buy a new car and the color red is a must, but the dealer says he has blue, that would be a no-go.

4. Give a weight (score each item 1 to 10, for example) for each want. Making a comparison by looking at alternatives in pairs can help with relative weights.

5. Score each alternative and decide.

Here is an example.

1. Prepare a decision statement that includes not only the desired result but also the action required. An example is, "Should the church purchase the used van from Friendship Church, purchase a used van from the car dealer, or purchase a new van?"

2. Define the strategic requirements (the must-haves):
   V-6 engine
   Not been in accident
   No required repairs
   16-passenger capacity
   Warranty

3. Then define the operational objectives (wants):
   Domestic model

Side steps already installed
Tires rated to last at least 20,000 miles
Built-in GPS
4. Rank the objectives and assign relative weights.

Objective	Weight
Want a	4
Want b	6
Want c	7
Want d	2
[Add other objectives as needed]	

List options and alternatives. Generate as many potential courses of action as possible whether they are immediately possible or not.

Score each option. Eliminate any option that does not fit the must-haves. For example, the van from Friendship Church carries twelve passengers, not sixteen, so it is eliminated.

Discuss and evaluate each option one by one, rating it against each want on a scale of 1 to 10.

Next, multiply the weight of the objective by the decision option score to calculate the weighted score.

Objective	Weight	Decision Option 1 Score	Weighted Score
Want a	4	4	16
Want b	6	6	36
Want c	7	6	42
Want d	2	7	14
Total Weighted Score for Option 1			108

If your team is considering six options, repeat the process for each decision option.

Choose the top two or three options and consider potential problems or negative effects of each.

Option/Alternative	Potential Problem or Negative Consequence
A–Used van at car dealer	Warranty not as long as new car
B–Used van at car dealer	Repair could be higher

Consider each alternative against all of the negative effects. One at a time again, rate alternatives against adverse effects, scoring for probability and significance.

Adverse Effect	Probability	Significance	Weighted Score
A	6	4	24
B	8	8	64
Adversity Rating for Alternative 1			88

Analyze the weighted score versus the adversity rating for each option and choose the high-scoring one.

5. Consider the winning option (best scoring) against each negative consequence and suggest a plan of action to minimize the adverse effects. Prepare a project plan to implement the decision.

As was mentioned when describing the KT method, this model utilizes a rational approach, with data and a human perspective. A human perspective means that, even though you go through the analysis process and get a recommendation for the decision based on your analysis, you still evaluate to make sure nothing was missed. Figure 4.3 is an evaluation checklist to assist you.

Figure 4.3. Evaluation Checklist

Questions	Yes/No
Have you challenged the information and assumptions?	
Does the solution solve the real problem?	
Is the problem permanently solved (as opposed to temporary)?	
Does the solution have the intended effect?	
Have all consequences, negative and positive, of the solution been well thought out?	
Has the team argued both sides, positive and negative?	
Has the solution accomplished all that is possible?	
Is the solution cost-effective and justifiable for the short and long term?	
Will we get buy-in from the congregation and/or community?	
Does the solution cause problems (for seniors, children, community)? If yes, discuss the issues.	
Is there any new information we need to consider? If yes, discuss the new information.	

If any of the first nine questions is answered no, or if either or both of the last two questions is answered yes, the team should discuss a plan of action.

Conclusion

To conclude this chapter, a comment made by Carl F. George comes to mind. George is director of the Pasadena-based Charles E. Fuller Institute of Evangelism and Church Growth. In this role he spends time with individual churches and pastors who have requested help. He reminds us as pastoral leaders that "virtually every decision has a moral aspect, but there are also other modes to consider: effective versus ineffective, good versus best, safe versus risky."[5] Churches are human-based organizations, like the many other organizations where we work. People have differing opinions, traditions, customs, and sometimes strong feelings about how things are to be done. Tensions arise as a result, making decisions stimulating, thought-provoking, and at times challenging. Thus, how we make decisions, the data we use (or choose not to use), who we as leaders involve, and the spiritual foundation of the decision-makers is paramount. Using data for decision-making in your church is about understanding your community's and congregation's needs and then matching those needs with relevant ministry solutions. Using data in the strategic planning of ministry helps pastors understand the church's people and the community it serves and gives leaders the ability to lead more effectively in the future.

Notes

1. "Guidelines for Using the Nominal Group Technique," produced by the New England Regional Leadership Program and posted by the Center for Rural Studies for public use, https://www.uvm.edu/crs/resources/nerl/group/a/meet/Exercise7/b.html.

2. Patty Mulder, "Kepner Tregoe Method," ToolsHero, 2012, https://www.toolshero.com/problem-solving/kepner-tregoe-method/.

3. Charles H. Kepner and Benjamin B. Tregoe, *The New Rational Manager*, updated ed. (Princeton, NJ: Princeton Research Press, 1997), is a critically acclaimed book that describes how Kepner's and Tregoe's thinking processes have led to successful business outcomes for more than fifty years. From troubleshooting major IT system outages to building effective leadership, KT rational processes are used by corporations, executives, managers, systems professionals, engineers, and other leaders.

4. Kepnor and Tregoe, *The New Rational Manager*, 164.

5. Carl F. George, "Making Decisions," Christianity Today, https://www.christianitytoday.com/pastors/leadership-books/leaders/ldlib12-9.html. George's wisdom is gained from thirteen years in the pastorate (University Baptist Church, Gainesville, Florida),

consulting work with more than three dozen denominations, postgraduate study in sociology, and wide self-education.

Resources

CDC. "Gaining Consensus Among Stakeholders through the Nominal Group Technique," No. 7. Updated August 2018. https://www.cdc.gov/healthyyouth/evaluation/pdf/brief7.pdf.

Conyne, Robert K., Jeri L. Crowell, and Mark D. Newmeyer. *Group Techniques: How to Use Them More Purposefully*. Upper Saddle River, NJ: Prentice Hall, 2007.

Decision Making Confidence. "Kepner Tregoe Decision Making: The Steps, The Pros and The Cons." https://www.decision-making-confidence.com/kepner-tregoe-decision-making.html.

Kepner, Charles H., and Benjamin B. Tregoe. *The New Rational Manager: An Updated Edition for a New World*. Princeton, NJ: Princeton Research Press, 2013.

Kepner Tragoe Inc. https://www.kepner-tregoe.com/

CHAPTER 5

Human Resource Management

What Is Human Resource Management?

Human resource management (HRM) is an integral component of many corporate, as well as nonprofit, organizations. Church members who work outside the church know it well; it is the organization that is central to such activities as hiring, recruiting, training, and benefits. Depending on the size of the church, it may or may not have an HRM function or staff member with that function. Nonetheless, it is critical. Why? People—human resources—are the most important assets of any organization, including the church; a local church cannot be successful without effectively managing people, including those who are hired and those who are volunteers.

With this as a foundation, let's start by defining human resource management. HRM is "the term used to describe formal systems devised for the management of people within an organization. The responsibilities of a human resource manager fall into three major areas: staffing, employee compensation and benefits, and defining/designing work."[1]

Fundamentally, the purpose of HRM is to maximize the productivity of an organization by optimizing the effectiveness of its people, both employees and volunteers. Regardless of organization type—church or secular—this mandate is unlikely to change in any fundamental way, despite the aggressive pace of change in the world of work and church. As Edward L. Gubman, a human resource consultant, points out, "human resources needs to acquire, develop, and retain talent, . . . and it must align the workforce with the business plan, despite the fluid, fast-changing environment of today's strategic business planning."[2] This principle applies to the church as well.

Thus, pastors need a solid grounding in managing human resources within the church. Successful implementation of any ministries, new ministry strategies, or even new, innovative ideas principally depends on acceptance by the people involved, both staff and volunteers. Without their acceptance no new ministry can survive, however useful it may be. Under these circumstances, the role of the pastor's leadership of HRM cannot be overemphasized.

Many church members can highlight cases in which important and useful ministry ideas failed mainly due to lack of acceptance by the people. This does not mean people were antagonistic to new ideas or strategy. But it does potentially imply that lack of proper education and training leads to misconceptions which in turn lead to failure to understand and accept important ministry innovations.

HRM is a vital part of every church. Churches often have staff, which can be at a minimum a hired secretary, in addition to the pastor. Furthermore, committee leaders and members (volunteers) are an integral part of the staff that assures organizational success. Depending on the size of the church, a church staff can include hired assistant pastors, teachers, choir directors, or facility workers. To underpin an effective church organization, the pastor in his or her role as chief executive must have a solid understanding in a number of important areas. The pastor and HR team (sometimes called the personnel committee in some Baptist churches or staff-parish relations committee in the Methodist Church) is responsible for diverse aspects of each employee's vocation and calling, from recruitment to hiring to various aspects of their job, while employed by the church. An effective church human resource committee or staff executes church policies and procedures and assists the pastor in keeping paid and volunteer personnel motivated and productive as they "equip the saints for the work of ministry, for building up the body of Christ" (Ephesians 4:12, ESV).

With this in mind, there are five basic skills of church HRM in which pastors should gain proficiency.

Hiring and Recruitment

The pastor must be adept at coaching church staff in hiring and recruiting new employees and volunteer staff. Identifying, recruiting, interviewing, and hiring a high-performing staff and volunteer group (committee members and committee leaders from inside or outside the church) is essential for the long-term achievement of the church. This includes creating policies and procedures for hiring and recruiting, as well as developing and documenting job descriptions, roles, and responsibilities. Teaching these skills to all of the church's leaders is also critical for the future of the church organization. This component of the HRM role also includes being knowledgeable and applying the various legal statutes and guidelines (local, state, and federal) associated with hiring (or firing) of employees.

Compensation and Benefits

To retain and motivate employees and organizational volunteers, the local church, with executive leadership by the pastor, will create, administer, and improve its compensation and benefits and recognition system. Retaining excellent staff and volunteers depends on many factors. Fair, consistent, and adequate pay and benefits are critical factors that will ultimately determine how your employees feel about the way the church cares for its people and their livelihood. Compensation, benefits, and recognition impact the likelihood that they will remain with the church long-term. Thus, working with denominational or local professional resources in crafting an effective compensation and recognition system and determining the best benefits package for all church employees is a mandatory skill for any pastor.

Training and Development

I recall a discussion I once had with one of the lay leaders of a church that I pastored. Our discussion was related to why some churches seemed to be more effective in making disciples for Christ. In particular we were discussing a church that seemed to be out in the middle of nowhere, yet it had a strong and vital congregation. Our conclusion was that there was strong, vision-oriented leadership at the church. As a result, the staff of the church had training and development that fostered everyone focusing and leading based on the mission and vision of the church.

For the pastor to achieve this result requires training and development skills. For staff development and mission-oriented leadership, this skill is vital for the pastor. The ability to create training programs, either made for the staff or with the assistance of available resources, can help a pastor align the church staff to church ministry objectives or resolve performance problems. In the long term, this will yield important benefits for the church. Instructional design skills, as well as facilitation and presentation skills, result in training and development programs that grow employees' and volunteers' skills and capabilities.

New skills and capabilities underpin a church's ability to produce measurable ministry results. For example, churches often do projects. Some achieve the expected results; others overrun their budgets. Yet, there are times when the expected results are not achieved, and the team is left asking, "How can we prevent this on a future project?" Training and development provide a way for staff to gain talent in program evaluation and review techniques so they can ask important questions such as "What did we do well? What can we improve? and What should we not do again?" Furthermore, training is often required for staff to gain valuable employee feedback so that there is the possibility of strategically improving the quality of all ministry efforts and programs.

Performance Management

To achieve the results of making disciples for Christ, fulfilling the mission of the church, and achieving the local church's ministry vision, the church organization and the staff, paid or volunteer, must have measureable objectives. These are often referred to as key results indicators. A pastor's ability to manage effectively the performances of church ministry projects and employees is an integral part of the HRM function of the church. Establishing and implementing a complete performance improvement process is an essential leadership skill. Implementing such things as a performance review process, maintaining it, and effectively monitoring its implementation are critical yet challenging responsibilities. The ability to teach staff and coach church leaders on how to use the performance management system is also an important function of church HRM and the pastor, who is the chief executive for system performance and effectiveness.

Volunteer Management

Bill Hybels, the founding and former senior pastor of Willow Creek Community Church in South Barrington, Illinois, one of the most-attended churches in North America, makes an important observation about church leadership and volunteerism:

> Leaders sometimes feel guilty asking people to serve in the church. But the church is made up of car dealers and stockbrokers, bankers and bricklayers, teachers and plumbers—and while the best of them are doing all they can to give God glory in their workplaces, few of them derive ultimate satisfaction from their jobs. Leaders have been given the unspeakable privilege of inviting people like these to participate in the thrill of knowing that the Creator God has used them to touch the lives of others spiritually.[3]

The responsibility of managing those who volunteer in the church is critical. And at the same time, one of the biggest challenges churches, large and small, face is the assemblage of volunteers to serve within the church and outside the church walls in the community. Millions of Christians who gather together every Sunday morning are eager to reach out, serve in areas where their passions lie, and share their faith with others. The challenge for pastors is how best to recruit and organize volunteers for ministry effectiveness. The Vanderbloemen Search Group, a church consultancy firm, highlights a few things that church pastors and leaders need to be aware of when approaching the challenge of creating a culture of volunteerism and service: barriers, fear, and experience. Within experience, Vanderbloemen includes making a contribution, finding friends, and having fun.[4]

Volunteer management also requires much more than getting people to sign up. Depending on the size of the church, there will be a requirement for a volunteer management system or strategy. For example, if you have a large volunteer base and children are a prominent part of your ministry, there is a requirement for risk management. Such a system helps the church ensure that volunteers, including church members, are vetted. Churches need to maintain data on volunteers and need accurate volunteer logs to determine when a volunteer has entered or left your facility, for example.

Again, a church's lifeblood is often its volunteers. As Thomas Bandy, president of Thriving Church Consulting, LLC, writes, "Churches need to learn the absolute number one reason why volunteers give up, walk out, and never come back. They simply will not allow themselves to suffer abuse. All it takes is one bullying, mean, critical, offensive church matriarch or patriarch to treat a volunteer disgracefully. Not only will that volunteer quit, but the word will quickly spread that a church is not able, or unwilling, to protect their volunteers."[5] Such a situation will not bode well for volunteer recruiting or discipleship making.

Conclusion

As I close this chapter, I am reminded of the apostle Paul, who said, "For just as the body is one and has many members, and all the members of the body, though many, are one body, so it is with Christ" (1 Corinthians 12:12, NRSV). People—staff and volunteers—make up the church and execute its ministry. Each person's part is as equally important as another's. Each person must work in harmony with each other. Each person must take accountability for his or her responsibilities in working in concert with the rest of the congregation (the body of Christ). To lead God's people in doing this, human resource management is critical.

Notes

1. "Human Resource Management," Inc., https://www.inc.com/encyclopedia/human-resource-management.html.

2. Edward L. Gubman, "The Gauntlet Is Down," *Journal of Business Strategy*, Vol. 17, Issue 6, (November 1, 1996).

3. Bill Hybels, "Growing Your Church's Volunteer Base," Christianity Today, August 3, 2016, http://www.christianitytoday.com/pastors/2016/july-web-exclusives/growing-your-churchs-volunteer-base.html.

4. "How to Recruit Church Volunteers & Create a Culture of Service," Vanderbloemen, June 4, 2013, *https:*//www.vanderbloemen.com/blog/how-to-recruit-church-volunteers-create-a-culture-of-service.

5. Thomas Bandy, "Why Churches Can't Get (and Keep) Volunteers," Ministry Matters, September 3, 2013, http://www.ministrymatters.com/all/entry/4217/why-churches-cant-get-and-keep-volunteers. Bandy is an internationally recognized consultant, conference speaker, and leadership coach for Christian organizations and faith-based nonprofits.

CHAPTER 6

Financial Decision-Making

A standard requirement in any MBA program will be a course in finance and financial management. A course in corporate finance is the typical introductory class. For one who wants to delve into more specifics of finance, topics such as international financial markets, managerial finance, financing of governments in the urban economy, and management of investment, among others, are available. Students can also choose an MBA program with a specialty in finance.

This chapter serves as an introduction to finance through the lens of the church. It will cover some of the theory and practice of financial decision-making within the church, as well as other relevant topics. We will not attempt to cover the whole subject. Finance is a vast topic, more than can be taught in a single chapter. For example, if one looks at the description of the corporate finance course in the Wharton School MBA program, one will note that prerequisites for this class include basic courses in microeconomics and statistics as well as an introductory accounting course.[1] So, we want to provide an overview of the components of financial management and their relevance to the church and church decision-making. We will also provide some finance tools that can be applied in church financial management as well as a section about resources for further learning.

Financial Management and Ethical Behavior

Financial management, as defined by *Business Dictionary*, is "the planning, directing, monitoring, organizing, and controlling of the monetary resources of an organization."[2] More specifically, James

C. Van Horne and John M. Wachowicz, Jr., in *Fundamentals of Financial Management*, define it as the "acquisition, financing, and management of assets with some overall goal in mind."[3]

In the broader world of finance, there are professional organizations that set standards of practice, such as the Institute of Management Accountants. It has principles of ethical behavior that focus on such things as honesty, fairness, objectivity, integrity, credibility, and responsibility.

What is financial management for the church? As we think about this question, it is important to put this in the spiritual context. Dan Busby, who serves as president of the Evangelical Council for Financial Accountability (ECFA), states, "We're talking about God's resources that individuals and others give to the church to be used for kingdom purposes, and that would be a difference between the for-profit world and the church world. So the fact that we're dealing with kingdom resources in the church world would require us to step up to a higher level of integrity with respect to how those funds are handled."[4] For financial management in the church, we live to an even higher standard—the Word of God. Financial management in the church should be done with the highest possible integrity.

Principles of Financial Management

While a number of sources speak to financial management principles, both academic and practical, here are some basics that are pertinent to church leaders.

Don't Risk Without Significant Return

We live in a time where there have been numerous stories about financial mismanagement in the church, as well as in other areas of communities in which we live and serve. Therefore, it is imperative that church leaders recognize the importance of risk management as an essential part of organizational management and leadership.

But what does proper risk management look like, and whose responsibility is it? Many in the church may assume that the pastor and staff are the only ones responsible for this. Such an approach to church financial risk management is problematic. As Michael E. Batts, a former chairman of the board of the ECFA, points out, "Church leaders are typically consumed with day-to-day operating activities and decisions—the 'tyranny of the urgent.' As a result, they frequently do not have, or take, the time to step back and proactively assess organizational risks and address them proactively."[5]

Thus, pastors must come to grips with the fact that they as leaders must be proactive in assuring the integrity of church financial management. In the text below are some key insights for risk management. First, however, a definition is helpful:

> Risk management is the process of protecting the tangible and intangible assets of your church or ministry. Tangible assets are physical properties, such as cash, buildings, furnishings, sound systems, computer equipment, etc. Intangible assets are the reputation, public image, or "brand" of the ministry. Intangible assets are also the people who attend the church, its staff, and its volunteers.[6]

Risk management, or protecting a church's assets, requires focused and careful planning. In our local churches, leaders and members want assurances that the good of the church and those it serves are in line with the will of Christ. There are few, if any, areas in which members want assurances as in the area of church finances. Thus, every church, regardless of size, should consider it important to have proper systems and procedures in place to receive, tally, and deposit contributions; to manage and govern the accounts related to these contributions; to execute disbursement of the funds through a careful, faithful, accurate, and documented budgeting process; and ultimately to disburse them for purposes that have been approved by the church's members and/or leaders through the budgeting process, policies, and procedures. This is an important undertaking. To promote these aims, consider the following examples of recommended content for a church financial policy document:

- Biblical basis
- Unrestricted gifts
- Budget presentation
- Review of financial records
- Accountable reimbursement plan[7]

Many resources regarding financial risk management are available. A good starting point would be denominational offices. For independent churches, other resources include the Nonprofit Risk Management Center (www.nonprofitrisk.org); a pamphlet called "ECFA Standards and Best Practices for Churches," published by the Evangelical Council for Financial Accountability; and a book, *Weeds in the Garden: The Growing Danger of Fraud Taking Root in the Church*, written by Verne Hargrave, a certified public accountant. Consider the following as you plan.

Develop a Realistic Church Budget

Church budgeting involves a master budget, which includes a separate capital and operating expense budget. Budgets render the ministry objectives into detailed plans (see the item below on planning).

Plan Ahead for Future Capital Needs

Capital is money used for an investment in such things as major equipment, mortgages, or facilities. Capital resources typically involve long-term financing for investment in these assets. Location of funds for both short- and long-term investment is required for sound financial management. Staying knowledgeable about resources (people and the services offered) from local banks can prove valuable.

Appoint or Elect Quality Leaders
Financial management requires competence, integrity, flexibility in dealing with the unknowns, and planning for the future. Dedicated, committed, competent finance leaders, including your finance team, are valuable for managing the Lord's resources. Always try to get a skilled and Spirit-led person for this role.

Monitor and Evaluate Financial Data
The ideas of monitoring and evaluating point to the need to assure that financial management is going according to plan and is done correctly and ethically. Church financial management should be more than a one-person task; there is great advantage in the model of a finance committee. Patricia Lotich, founder of Smart Church Management, recommends eleven things the church finance committee should do in order to lead responsible management and stewardship of church finances.

1. Revenue Projections—It is difficult to budget without having a realistic idea of how much money will be available. Take a realistic approach to projecting revenues by analyzing historical giving, attendance patterns, and average member donations.
2. Budgeting Process—The budget committee establishes the global budget based on revenue projections and allocates dollars to individual departments. The individual [ministry team leaders] are responsible for creating their own budget estimates based on church strategy, goals, and allocated resources. Allowing individual [ministry team leaders] to prepare their own budget estimates makes them more accountable, accurate, and reliable.

3. Budget Review—A budget is simply an itemized allotment of funds and require[s] monitoring. This committee should be monitoring the budget every month, reviewing the actual dollars that came in, and the actual dollars that went out, and analyzing any variances.

4. Emergency Funding—Even the best of budget planning can go awry when an unexpected major expense arises. To offset this, allocate a percentage of budget dollars to emergency funding. Keep this fund growing year after year so those unanticipated emergencies can be managed without impacting the rest of the budget.

5. Financial Reporting—Systematic reporting helps the church see how it is performing financially. Create monthly or quarterly reports and keep church leadership apprised of spending and budget variances. If there is an effort to raise building funds, show dollars that are available for the project and what percentage of funds have been raised. If there is a focus to pay down church debt, report on that also.

6. Good Stewardship—Churches rely on the generous donations of its members to do what they do. Being good stewards of those funds is a basic responsibility of the church board and finance committee. This team of people should challenge any spending that does not support the church mission, vision, or strategy.

7. Safeguarding Church Assets—The board along with the finance committee are responsible for ensuring that there are good financial controls with church assets. This committee should be writing cash-handling policies and auditing the process of anyone who handles church money. . . . If you think embezzlement in the church is not common, think again.

8. Ensuring Profit Margin—Profit margins are how nonprofit organizations grow their capital. Since nonprofit organizations can't take profits out of the organization, they invest any dollars that are above expenses back into the organization. For instance, if a church that brings in $500,000 budgets for a 5% profit margin, they will be saving $25,000 a year that can be reinvested into

church facilities. All church budgets should include a percentage that is designated as a profit margin.

9. Debt Management—It is difficult to get a church up and running without racking up some debt. However, a church is limited in what it can do if it is debt-ridden. The finance committee should have a strategy for paying down debt and that should be part of the budget.

10. Member Financial Teaching—Church members are only as giving as their personal finances allow. The finance committee can influence members by offering teaching in personal finance, budgeting, and common sense to finances. Help members get a handle on their own personal finances and giving will inevitably increase.

11. Manager Budget Training—Churches that employ people to manage various departments within the church should use the finance committee to help train church leaders on how to manage their budget, how to read and interpret financial reporting statements, and how to address departmental budget variances. This committee should develop this training and create a simple process to help ministry team leaders become financially literate.[8]

A key lesson Lotich points out is that "a church finance committee is the financial think-tank for a church. Develop a finance committee that is committed to budgeting, monitoring and controlling how church funds are spent and your church will have the necessary resources to fulfill its mission, vision and strategy."[9]

Plan for the Unexpected

Despite all of our best efforts, churches face unforeseen emergencies. Remember that air conditioning unit that failed in the middle of summer? It is important to save enough money or have a fund to be able to face unexpected repairs, such as for the van, bus, facility, or parsonage. Increasing the amount of money you save when giving is higher can help manage the cost when the church faces financial challenges, ensuring that unexpected financial exposure does not derail your long-term ministry goals and the church's financial security.

Consider the Risk Associated with the Venture
Churches are sometimes involved in new ventures; for example, a church might decide to build an addition, buy a second property, or purchase another facility in order to start a second worship campus. In such cases, analysis of the operational risk, long-term financial health of the congregation (financial model), and other implications should be performed to determine the risk of the venture. This also may be a time to consider using a consultant.

Remember That Nothing Happens Without a Plan
Sometimes we as leaders and laity feel like it takes a lot of work to plan, but planning is a requirement in managing church finances. Things don't have to be perfect in order to do church financial planning, and financial planning is not just something that large churches do. Planning is a vital step for all churches.

Use Cash as a Basis for New Project Decisions
In the corporate world, it is important to have a certain amount of cash available. In this case, cash is liquid assets, not money you can get from a bank (debt). Cash is critical to financial management. New projects in the church should not always be based on getting capital from a bank. If a loan is always required, you might want to rethink your financial health.

Continuously Educate Yourself
New knowledge is continually being created. Even for pastors or church financial leaders, it is good to read financial periodicals, books, and denominational communications to understand

current thinking on finance, investing strategies, and opportunities that benefit the church.

Conclusion

In this chapter, we have not attempted to be professors of finance. There are a great number of other components to church financial management to discuss that space does not allow for. Some of these items are understanding money from an economic perspective (authorities and limitations, types and restrictions, obligated versus budgeted expenses, capital and revolving accounts, etc.); fundamentals of accounting; return on investment (ROI); contract financial management (using consultants); and an in-depth look at budgeting (e.g., bottom up, top down, roll over, historical, zero-based budgeting, multi-year considerations, and inflation forecasting, just to name a few). For those who would like resources for more study, we have listed some additional readings in the resources section.

We have made reference to the need for churches to follow their financial management policies and procedures. Sensing that many churches will have policies and procedures around building use, safe sanctuary, and maintenance, but not necessarily financial management, we have included an example of a financial management policy (see appendix 2). To achieve solid church financial management, having policies and procedures are important as we follow the leadership of the Holy Spirit. The Word of God teaches about financial management: "Suppose one of you wants to build a tower. Won't you first sit down and estimate the cost to see if you have enough money to complete it? For if you lay the foundation and are not able to finish it, everyone who sees it will ridicule you, saying, 'This person began to build and wasn't able to finish'" (Luke 14:28-30, NIV).

Notes

1. "MBA Course Descriptions," The Wharton School, https://fnce.wharton.upenn.edu/programs/mba/course-descrip

tions/. The Wharton School is the business school of the University of Pennsylvania, one of the premier MBA programs.

2. "Financial Management," Business Dictionary, http://www. businessdictionary.com/definition/financial-management.html.

3. James C. Van Horne and John M. Wachowicz, Jr., *Fundamentals of Financial Management*, 13th ed. (New York: Pearson Education, 2009), 1.

4. Dan Busby, "For-Profit vs. Church Financial Management," *Church Finance Today*, December 6, 2016, https://www.church lawandtax.com/blog/2016/december/for-profit-vs-church-finan cial-management.html.

5. Michael E. Batts, "Building a Culture of Risk Management," Managing Your Church, September 25, 2012, https://www.church lawandtax.com/blog/2012/september/building-culture-of-risk-management.html.

6. "Church Risk Management in 5 Simple Steps," AG Financial Solutions, https://www.agfinancial.org/blog/bid91200church-risk-management-in-5-simple-steps/. AG Solutions has more than seventy years of experience in providing church financial solutions, management, and risk management.

7. Keith Hamilton, "A Model Church Financial Policy," Lifeway, January 1, 2014, https://www.lifeway.com/en/articles/a-model-church-financial-policy.

8. Patricia Lotich, "11 Things Your Church Finance Committee Should Be Doing," Smart Church Management, December 9, 2015, https://smartchurchmanagement.com/church-finance-com mittee/. Smart Church Management is a church management consulting company that offers services to help the local church develop systems and processes to support church growth. Lotich is an MBA and Certified Manager of Quality and Organizational Excellence through the American Society for Quality.

9. Ibid.

Resources

Books

Batts, Michael E., and Richard R. Hammar. *Church Finance: The Complete Guide to Managing Ministry Resources*. Carol Stream, IL: Christianity Today International, 2015.

Boatright, Vickey, and Lisa London. *Church Accounting: The How To Guide for Small and Growing Churches (The Accountant Beside You)*. Sanford, NC: Deep River Press, 2014.

Crockett, Lee Ann. *Preventing Fraud in Church Accounting: Common Problems and Practical Solutions That Church Leaders Can't Afford to Ignore*. 2018.

Risk Management

Stewardship. "Is Risk Management Right for Churches?" September 2017. https://www.stewardship.org.uk/downloads/brief ingpapers/is-risk-managment-right-for-churches.pdf. This resource includes tools for a church to conduct a risk assessment if your denominational group does not provide one.

Key Financial Management Terms

NYS Society of CPAs. "Accounting Terminology Guide—Over 1,000 Accounting and Finance Terms." https://www.nysscpa.org/ professional-resources/accounting-terminology-guide.

CHAPTER 7

Operations

What is operations management? The operations management function gives the leader the opportunity to apply expertise, strong leadership skills, ability to link people, and organizational performance and workflow processes to ensure optimal efficiency. Organizations of all sizes and types are looking to continuous improvement methods and strategies to manage costs and expenses, operate efficient facilities, and meet the increasing needs of the customer base (from a ministry perspective, think local church and community) as it seeks to provide service or products to its marketplace. Most MBA programs offer a course in this topic.

With this in mind, operations management focuses on making sure an organization runs as efficiently as possible. In other words, in this position, pastors would use professional expertise and analytical skills to manage resources—facilities, procurement, planning, human resources, technology, and processes—to help the organization succeed. Operations management is about balancing and figuring out how to operate all functions of the organization effectively.

In summary, the simplest definition of operations management is overseeing and controlling the day-to-day operations of an organization—nonprofit, church, small business, manufacturing company, computer data center—that sells goods or provides a service.

Why Operations Management Is Important to the Church

Operations management is typically not a term associated with ministry or pastoral leadership. Nonetheless, it has a function in the church. While in a corporate setting operations management is focused on the output or service of the organization, in the church the output is the various ministries it provides to the community. For example, Sunday worship services are an output. The church's educational program is an output. For congregations that have food pantries or clothing ministries, these too would be considered output. Furthermore, any of the front-facing activities and functions a church provides to keeps itself visible to the congregation and community would also be considered outputs. These are things like social media, ministry productions, music and musical performances, print media and advertising, and special day services. Thus, when the church organization's operations run smoothly and are under good management, the overall function and departments in the organization should operate effectively. When not, the opposite is the likely result—the organization's operations are managed improperly.

Let us share this example. Churches, as well as any organization, have human resources. This includes the functions of hiring, and, as necessary, soliciting and training volunteers. It also includes working with appropriate organizations to develop job descriptions, posting the job, new employee orientation, and job training. This is pertinent regardless of whether there are hired resources or volunteers.

When the overall operation of the organization runs effectively, the organization and its staff more easily get a reputation of one that is good to work for, has a good work environment, or does good things for the community. This translates to jobs being easier to fill, volunteer interest being higher, and less turnover due to work or organizational issues. Even the development of job descriptions becomes less of a chore since the organization's workplace environment is healthy. When the opposite is the case—poor operations function—the human resource management function becomes challenged. For example, high turnover, difficulty attracting quality candidates for hire, and lack of interested volunteers (internally and externally) become the consequence. The result to the church: higher cost of operating the HR function in the church and likely an overworked and frustrated staff.

As we mentioned at the outset of this section, operations management is typically not a term associated with pastoral leadership, or even studied by pastors and church leaders in seminary. But consider some aspects of organizational function that church leaders need to have insight in:

- How can I create a sustainable organization?
- What is the product or service that I am dealing with?
- When the church needs to purchase resources, how do I determine the best options for procurement?
- How do learning curves and performance of staff and volunteers impact the success of my organization?
- Facility location and layout are important to the success of ministries. How do I know what is best?
- What are the requirements and how shall the church manage security operations?
- How do the local laws and regulations impact the church and current or future ministries we may want to implement?
- How are concepts like quality assurance, metrics, data analysis, forecasting, demographics, and lean management relevant to ministry success? Do they apply to me as a pastor or leader and to the operations of our church?
- How do we schedule church employees and volunteers?
- How do we integrate the financial needs of our congregation into everyday approaches?
- How do we manage technology and information management in the church context?[1]

With this in mind, let's compare operations management from the contexts of church leadership and manufacturing leadership (table 7.1).

Table 7.1. Comparison of Manufacturing and Church Operations

Manufacturing Organization	Church Organization
Tangible product	Intangible product
Product can be inventoried	Product cannot be inventoried
Low customer contact	High customer contact
Longer response time	Short response time
Capital intensive	People intensive
Medium product appeal response time	High product appeal response time
Facility is main capital asset	Facility is main capital asset

Concepts and Tools of Operations Management

As mentioned above, the operations management function helps the organization operate efficiently. Concepts, skills, and tools related to operations management are both strategic and tactical, and as such can be applied to a multitude of organizations. Here is a sample.

Policies and Procedures

Policies and procedures allow church leaders to guide operations without constant intervention. And constant intervention equates to detraction from the church's mission. In order to understand why policies and procedures are so important to the church, let's start with definitions:

> A 'Policy' is a predetermined course of action, which is established to provide a guide toward accepted business strategies and objectives. In other words, it is a direct link between an organization's 'Vision' and their day-to-day operations. Policies identify the key activities and provide a general strategy to decision-makers on how to handle issues as they arise. … The ultimate goal of every 'Procedure' is to provide the reader with a clear and easily

understood plan of action required to carry out or implement a policy.[2]

Why are policies and procedures important to a church? Patricia Lotich provides important insights: "As a church grows, internal processes and systems grow with it, creating the need to write things down. Doing so in a detailed policy and procedure manual can help to ensure that the services that the church provides can consistently maintain the level of quality that the church hopes to achieve."[3]

Project Management

In manufacturing companies, project managers spend considerable amounts of time planning projects—a new product line, a new process, new suppliers, or design and build of new technology, for example. In the same way, church projects include such things as implementing Vacation Bible School, starting a new senior respite ministry, planning a church anniversary, or updating or renovating the buildings. Yet, many times, church projects are not implemented with formal project planning. Formal implementation of project management in the church fosters more efficient use of resources, planning to meet schedules and achieving the project objectives. Thus, in operations management, project management is an essential tool. Chapter 12 provides more details on managing projects in ministry. In addition, for a more in-depth understanding of project management in the church, see *Managing Projects in Ministry*. The bottom line is that it is important to go through everything—from start to finish—needed to complete the project. Create a timeline for it and track the details required to perform long-term scheduling and planning as you work to achieve the project goal.

Quality Control

Quality control is a term often used when there is a product being made; it is what an auto manufacturer would do. But regardless of the organization, quality control is all about setting and maintaining an established standard to measure the result of your product or service. A church can feel free to criticize the quality control data, and, if necessary, establish improved or more realistic expectations. Additionally, the church can conduct regular surveys with attendees to determine whether ministry goals are being met.

Team Building

Though churches are made up of many individuals with differing skill sets, the organization functions best when everyone is working toward the same goal. In the case of the church, everything we do should be anchored in the call that Jesus gave us in Matthew 28:19: "go and make disciples." As Rick Warren, pastor of Saddleback Church, emphasizes, "The success of your ministry depends largely on developing a strong team with a deep sense of team spirit. I've witnessed the incredible power of a unified team to create growth and have counseled many churches who weren't growing because their team members worked as individuals and not as a team."[4] As leaders, we must remember that Jesus designed the church to work as a team, as we learn from Romans 12:4-8. With this foundation, here are biblical insights for team building.

■ **Ecclesiastes 4:9** (NKJV): "Two are better than one, [b]ecause they have a good reward for their labor." Many great and important achievements are attained by teamwork. The recent United States women's World Cup win, like any great sports victory, was achieved by teamwork. So it is in the church. Christ gives us the ultimate example of teamwork in ministry. He did not do everything by himself. He created a team (the disciples) so that his mission would be accomplished long-term.

■ **1 Peter 4:10** (NKJV): "As each one has received a gift, minister it to one another, as good stewards of the manifold grace of God."

One of the great benefits of a team is that each member has valuable and differing talents that contribute to team success. It is important for church leaders, including the pastor, to be conduits for bringing out the best of each team member—laity, volunteers, and staff—so that the church as a whole maximizes for the good of the kingdom of God.

■ **Ephesians 4:11** (NRSV): "The gifts he gave were that some would be apostles, some prophets, some evangelists, some pastors and teachers." In my past role as a bi-vocational pastor, I was a manager of manufacturing. Under my leadership were multiple departments—like production, engineering, and others. Each of these departments required a leader, and as such we then became a leadership team. Just as the apostle Paul reminds us, God also emphasized the importance of the ministry leadership team members (e.g., apostles, teachers, pastors), with each being accountable for specific contributions for the church and community ministry.

■ **Romans 15:5** (NKJV): "Now may the God of patience and comfort grant you to be like-minded toward one another, according to Christ Jesus." The team concept emphasizes the importance of each person contributing his or her gifts and skills and building a bond that allows it to function with like-mindedness. When this is the case, a strong team bond also results in each team member looking out for one another, as we are taught in Philippians 2:4 (CEV): "Care about them as much as you care about yourselves."

Formal Scheduling
With formal scheduling—not just an informal calendar on the wall—the church implements a formal system that allows the organization to set deadlines for overall goals and objectives throughout the year. By so doing, the church can track ministries or projects. Furthermore, leadership can require accurate progress reports so everyone involved is kept up-to-date. Scheduling can be

used in any church—small or large, and in all auxiliaries—and adapted to fit your needs.

Maintenance

Equipment and facility maintenance is important for any organization. For example, the heating, ventilation, and air conditioning systems are significant pieces of capital equipment in your facility. As such, they should be formally maintained and checked regularly. Any vehicles the church uses—buses in particular—should have the regularly scheduled oil changes and tire rotations according to the manufacturer's recommendations. Additionally, any other necessary maintenance should be performed to keep them in good operating condition. The church should have documented procedures for assuring this is managed effectively. If the work is to be done internally, standard operating procedures should be documented. If the work if contracted, there should be someone who assures that work is done properly.

Equally of importance for maintenance is the church information technology system. Computers and other hardware (printers, copiers, cameras, recording or duplication devices, and scanners) used in the church should be maintained properly, including updates to virus protection and systems for protecting personal data (this is especially critical if your church has a childcare center). Again, there should be documented policies and procedures, standard operating procedures, and defined roles and responsibilities. Maintenance calendars can be created to track all related tasks.

The Pastor's Role in Leading Operations Management

To help put operations management in context for the pastor, let us use an example of a pastor who is in the process of doing an evaluation to determine if his congregation should expand its campus. Currently the church has three services, and the facility is located in the heart of the community. They have parking lots as well as a shuttle service. Nonetheless, there is still a need for on-street partaking. Both the 9:30 a.m. and the 11:30 a.m. services are packed, including the balcony. A property is available in the same neighborhood where the church currently serves.

From an operations management perspective, here are a number of operations considerations this pastor and the church leadership staff likely will consider as they evaluate the need for expansion:

■ Should they build a new building or buy and renovate an existing facility?

■ If they decide to renovate an existing facility, what are the zoning ordinances?

■ Will there be a need for an expanded staff with a larger facility?

■ What is the cost to build new versus buy and renovate?

■ What floor layout should a renovated (or new) facility have to achieve the desired ambiance for worship?

■ What changes should be made to the current IT and AV infrastructure in the future facility?

■ What must be done to achieve facility security in a new location?

■ What new processes will be required during the build or renovate phase to allow for a continued high-quality worship experience until the new facility is ready for occupation?

■ What are community communication and marketing strategies required during this transition phase?

■ Will the expansion phase increase the workload on the staff, and, if so, what options for balance should be implemented to assure success?

■ What will be the legal considerations (both operational and design-based) in the new facility if there is a plan for a childcare?

The above list is not designed to be exhaustive. It seeks to show the breadth of factors that must be considered in church operations management. Furthermore, Mark Ashcraft and Bruce Woody of

Texas-based HH Architects, a firm that specializes in church campus master planning, emphasize the importance of operations management in designing worship space: "In Psalms 95:6, we read *Oh come, let us worship and bow down; let us kneel before the* LORD, *our Maker!* Next time you walk into a sanctuary (worship center), take a moment to reflect on what the space says to you. Does it help in creating the right atmosphere for receiving the message, or encouraging participation in worship?"[5] The point here is that operations efficiency requires purposeful leadership to achieve the vision God has put on the heart of the pastor.

Conclusion

In summary, the idea of considering operations management as part of church leadership might not seem obvious to many, but there are several benefits.

First, operations management helps to ensure that the church organization can remain relevant in an ever-changing environment. This means that leaders must be at the forefront of development and delivery of ministries that are effective and are running as efficiently as they possibly can. It also means fixing areas that are considered inefficient and ineffective.

Second, organizations often find that they are faced with resource constraint, including faithful church workers getting burned out. By employing operations management concepts that look at resource requirements and balance, the church can save itself from a situation that could result in its decline.

Third, the pastor's focus on operations management will help church leaders integrate into its norms the need for tools and strategies that address:

■ Performance measurement (how can we measure the results of our hospitality ministry in comparison with visitor attendance beyond their first visit?)

■ Performance improvement (how can we improve the VBS planned for 2019 compared with previous years—attendance, feedback from surveys, etc.?)

■ Capacity optimization (how well are facilities utilized for presenting new and innovative ministries that try to reach the unchurched?)

■ Cost reductions (how can we reduce our operating cost or spending in a way that allows us to expand our ministries?)

Ultimately, church operations management equips pastors to lead the church and to do the work of the church in a coherent, efficient, and comprehensive manner. It is the guidance provided by pastors and other church leaders as they use biblical, human, physical, and fiscal resources to move the church toward making disciples for Christ for the transformation of the world (Matthew 28:19).

Notes

1. "Why Study Operations Management?," ToughNickel, April 25, 2016, https://toughnickel.com/business/Why-Study-Operations -Management. The questions in this chapter are adapted from the list on ToughNickel.

2. Grant Welling, "Are Your Policies and Procedures a Barrier to Growing Your Company?," Pacific Crest Group, http://www.pcg services.com/are-your-policies-and-procedures-a-barrier-to-grow ing-your-company/.

3. Patricia Lotich, "Are Your Policies in Print? Or Left to Memory?," Smart Church Management, October 25, 2017, https://smart churchmanagement.com/7-reasons-write-church-procedures/.

4. Rick Warren, "8 Values of Teamwork That Keep a Church Healthy," Pastors.com, March 27, 2015, http://pastors.com/8-val ues-of-teamwork-that-keep-a-church-healthy/.

5. Mark R. Ashcraft and Bruce Woody, "How to ensure a truly engaging worship space, by design," Church Executive, April 1, 2018, https://churchexecutive.com/archives/engaging-spaces-11.

Resources

Articles

Cool, Tim. "9 Reasons Your Church Needs a Facility Management Professional." eSpace, November 18, 2016. https://www.espace.cool/2016/11/18/9-reasons-your-church-needs-a-facility-management-professional/.

Marmon, Pam. "7 Keys to a Smooth Church Transition." Christianity Today, August 31, 2017. https://www.christianityto day.com/pastors/2017/august-web-exclusives/7-keys-to-smooth-church-transition.html.

Rodgers, James. "Church Renovation Blind Spots." Christianity Today. https://www.christianitytoday.com/pastors/2009/fall/church -renovation-blind-spots.html.

"Worship Facilities Magazine." https://www.worshipfacilities.com.

Books

Cool, Tim. *Why Church Buildings Matter: The Story of Your Space*. Rainer Publishing, 2014.

Howell, Vincent Wyatt. *Managing Projects in Ministry*. Valley Forge, PA: Judson Press, 2017. Along with the book there are online resources, such as templates for project planning, project evaluation, and other tasks.

Moloney, Kris P., and Malene Little. *Defending the Flock: A Security Guide for Church Safety Directors*. CreateSpace, 2017.

Meredith, Jack R., and Scott M. Shafer. *Operations Management for MBAs*. 5th Ed. Hoboken, NJ: Wiley, 2012.

CHAPTER 8

Marketing

The world that we live in and the world that the church operates in is one that is closely linked to a market mentality. Each Sunday, our newspaper content seems to be fifty percent advertisements. Watch some television shows and they seem to run an advertisement every five minutes. And with our devices—phones, tablets, computers—the apps that we use on a regular basis have an integral marketing component. The same can be said for many internet searches and email programs. Even the church must face this reality, as these are tools of today. The purpose of all this is to keep the product or service visible in the minds of users and consumers. Christina Hamlett, a consultant specializing in audience analysis and message design, emphasizes that:

> Advertising helps to raise your target demographic's awareness of issues with which they may be unfamiliar as well as educate them on the related benefits of your product or service. A popular example of this is the health care industry. If, for instance, a consumer watches a television commercial in which someone describes aches and pains that are similar to those experienced by the viewer, the ad not only identifies a probable cause but suggests a potential remedy or treatment option to discuss with her doctor.[1]

In Hamlett's supposition, two thoughts are critical for any community church: raise awareness and educate on the benefits of the product or service. Like it or not, the ministry that we offer is viewed by those we are trying to reach as a product or service. Here is a case in point. A young family is new to your town, and they go to various churches to experience what the church has to offer—preaching, music, friendliness of the congregation, parking, services for children, and more. Once they evaluate each church and make a decision, they are in essence choosing one product over another. And not only that, before they dawn the door of your sanctuary, the family will likely do some pre-evaluation of your "product and services"—they will look at your website and social media presence (and if you don't have a website, your product has very limited market visibility).

This idea of raising awareness of the product or service is part of what MBA programs call marketing. Take a look at the curriculum of most MBA programs, and you likely will find a course titled "Marketing Management." In this chapter, we will discuss three components of marketing management: what marketing management is, why marketing is important to the church, and the pastor's role in church marketing.

What is Marketing Management?

A good starting point is to get a solid definition of marketing from the American Marketing Association (AMA). The AMA, which reaches nearly 1.3 million professionals focused on marketing globally, "is the world's largest marketing association, and the most relevant force and voice shaping marketing today." The AMA considers itself an essential community for marketers that inspires curiosity, debate, and connection. Here's AMA's definition of marketing: "Marketing is the activity, set of institutions, and processes for creating, communicating, delivering, and exchanging offerings that have value for customers, clients, partners, and society at large."[2]

Let us put this in context: Imagine you own a taco truck. What is the most valuable situation you can have? The answer is a crowd of hungry people lined up in front of your truck with money to buy your tacos! It doesn't matter how good your food or service is, it doesn't matter if you have the best price in town or how high your quality is; if you don't have hungry people lined up in front of your truck, willing and able to buy your product, then your business will struggle to succeed long-term. This same example applies to the church—people need to be hungry for the ministries at your church, and your congregation needs to attract people. It doesn't matter how good your choir or music ministry is, it doesn't matter if you have the most beautiful building in town, or high-quality sermons; if you don't have hungry people lined up, interested in attending and participating in your ministry programs (your product), then your church will struggle to succeed long-term.

Marketing is about figuring out how to create interest or buzz— excitement from a group of people so they will be "hungry people lined up in front of your taco truck" who want to come in and be part of your product, service, or ministry. A part of marketing is understanding what the people want and need and providing it. Consider how this recommendation from consulting firm One Sherpa could apply to ministry: "When deciding what sort of business you will create, or what type of product you will sell, make sure you do your homework so that you are supplying the products and services that people actually want. The best way to find this out is to simply ASK your customers."[3]

The marketing research faculty at Harvard Business School emphasize the importance of marketing. In reviewing this insight, implications for the church are evident.

> Marketing is critical for organic growth of a business and its central role is in creating, communicating, capturing and sustaining value for an organization. Marketing helps a firm in creating value by better understanding the needs of its customers and providing them with innovative products and services. This value is communicated through a

variety of channels as well as through the firm's branding strategy. Effective management of customers . . . allows the firm to capture part of the value it has created. Finally, by building an effective customer-centric organization a firm attempts to sustain value over time.[4]

In essence, marketing management seeks to addresses how to design and implement the best combination of marketing efforts to carry out the strategy of an organization—business or church—in the area of the community it seeks to target.

For the remainder of this chapter, we will specifically seek to develop the reader's understanding of why marketing is important to churches and how it can be beneficial to creating and delivering value to their congregations, communities, and broader ministry stakeholders (i.e., community organizations that collaborate with the church), and we will apply concepts and tools of marketing to such decisions as segmentation and targeting, branding, and promotion.

Why Marketing Is Important to the Church

Tim Schraeder, a former youth pastor at Alexandria Covenant Church, reminds us that "with every generation comes the challenge of communicating the unchanging, timeless message of the Gospel in a way that is relevant and compelling to the culture of its time. We live in a generation that has been influenced and shaped by marketing."[5] We as pastors must lead so that we can lead each generation into a relationship with our Lord and Savior Jesus Christ. We cannot expect them to come. We must interest them in learning that the church has something important to offer. This includes the messages we communicate verbally and non-verbally. It includes what impression we as pastors and the congregation have in the community. How we share the message about the Lord and the message of the church has implications—that is church marketing. As Schraeder points out, marketing has moved from promoting and selling to adding value and managing relationships. It's more than posters and bulletins and jingles; it's about making an emotional connection, sharing, and communicating captivating stories.

The church has something that the world needs: Jesus Christ. In business, marketing focuses on monetary gain (profit), whereas church marketing is for the greater good of society because the world truly must know that in Jesus we can have life and have it more abundantly. Life itself depends on it!

This is why marketing management is important to the church and why it is critical to the leadership capacity of the pastor.

Concepts and Tools of Marketing

When studying the function of marketing, a number of concepts are applied. These include the following:

- Product/service management
- Pricing
- Promotion
- Distribution
- Marketing information management (sometimes referred to as market research)
- Financing
- Selling

Not all of these apply to the church and church marketing management. For example, we contend that the pricing function has no relevance to the church. What we offer as the church is free, because Christ freely gave his life for us that we might have eternal life and have abundant life. On the other side, the idea of selling may seem irrelevant to the church, but we disagree. Before we can reach the children, the youth, the seniors, the singles, and the young married couples in the community—before we can attract them to our new ministries (selling)—we have determined the wants and needs (for example, does the community prefer a traditional or contemporary or simple worship) of the community (the customer base, in marketing terms) and are able to respond with the right ministry offerings. Therefore, church leaders, lay and pastor, from large urban churches to small rural churches, must recognize that if they want to reach the masses, they must be able to convince (sell) people in the community on the importance of the ministry and the church's message (the product, in marketing terms) they offer.

How do we apply this in the church? Let's first look at each of these concepts and its associated definition. Jeremy Bradley, an MBA graduate who works in the fields of educational consultancy and business administration, provides a helpful definition. We have adapted Bradley's definitions and put them in the context of the church.[6]

Distribution: Distribution is about deciding how you will build interest (sell) and get the ministry or program you are planning to the people whom you want to reach. Having an idea for a ministry or ministry product (e.g., DVD, book) is great, but if you aren't able to get that product to the customers you aren't going to have an effective ministry and reach others for Christ. Distribution can be as conceptualized as setting up tactics for circulation of ministry information in the part of town where your target audience is located. But in a world where church attendees overlap generations, cities, towns, and counties, and with an increasingly interconnected world (social media and communication), distribution more often than not now means that the church will need to take your ministry and services to the future disciples. This means they may not be interested in coming to your location or the brick-and-mortar building.

Financing: The reality is that many ministries require a budget. As a pastor, an important function of marketing a ministry is finding the money through giving, grants, loans, or church investments to finance the creation and advertising of your ministry.

Market research: Market research is about gathering information concerning your target ministry community. Who are the people? Where are the people you want to interest and reach with the ministry? Why should they be interested in the ministry at the church you lead as opposed to a ministry at another church? Answering these questions requires that you do some on-the-ground observation and data analysis of the community, its demographics, and other market trends that address community and business organizations (these may be opportunities for ministry collaboration). Take a look at the resource section for information regarding marketing research tools for ministry.

Ministry product management: Once you've determined the target group for the ministry (market) and set the ministry objectives, the goal becomes to manage effectively the ministry. Ministry product management involves ensuring that the church implements evaluation tools to determine if objectives are being met. For example, if a church wishes to kick off a new youth ministry in twelve months with activities and lessons that maintain the interest of the youth, there need to be tools for the leadership team to evaluate such questions as "What went well?", "Did we hit our attendance targets?", "Did we achieve advertising targets?", "What should we discontinue doing at the next session?", and "What was the feedback from the end-of-session feedback survey?"

In summary, ministry product management involves listening to ministry participants, responding to their needs and wants, and keeping your ministry fresh and appealing.

Promotion: Most of us have some acquaintance with the idea of product promotion. In the technology world, we see all sorts of product promotions, from the promotion of the latest smartphone to the services for cable television we sometime see in retail outlets. Advertising your ministry (the product of the church) is essential to attracting new participants and a new demographic, reaching the broader community, and keeping current members engaged. Furthermore, as community demographics and the overall social context of the church change, church leaders will want to respond appropriately by tailoring promotional messages to the appropriate conventional outlets (such as newspaper) and new media (such as Facebook, Snapchat, Twitter, and the church website) or by using a mix of the old and new.

Selling: While we tend to think of selling and marketing as being closely associated, selling is last on the list of the seven functions of marketing. This is because selling the ministry can happen only after the church has determined the interest, needs, and wants of its ministry community (customer base) and are able to respond with the appropriate ministries offered in the appropriate context and time frame. This isn't to say we should change the message of Christ. It is saying we as church leaders always need to determine the best way to reach the audience with the message. For example, musicians and record companies did not stop distributing music when the popular media switched from 45 rpm records or eight-track tapes; they adapted to music distribution via current channels, which now includes iTunes® or streaming.

One additional item that has marketing implications is the idea of church branding. Branding describes the image that a church hopes to instill in the minds of the community it serves or the audience it is attempting to reach. Steve Fogg, writing in "10 Common Branding Mistakes That Churches Make," says church branding is "also the language that is used, the visual look and feel around the logo, the kinds of photos used. Ultimately a successful church brand can be defined by the power and focus of the story you tell."[7]

The Pastor's Role in Leading Church Marketing

More than ever before, church marketing is an important part of church leadership. The marketing firm Church Marketing University contends that pastors and churches are falling into two primary categories: those that are tapping into the digital world and using new methods of communication to see church growth and those holding onto the tradition of the years past and still doing what they've always done and seeing limited growth, if any growth at all.

Marketing is important to the church. And as such, this is a subject that pastors must be familiar with. Jon Vaughan, a marketing champion at Group Publishing, helps churches build a healthy, thriving ministry that will meet the needs of the community long into the future. He emphasizes from a marketing perspective that pastors must assure clarity of their churches' messages, assure that their marketing messages also include a call for action ("What do you want me to do?"), keep websites and other social media current, understand the implications of their brands, and, lastly, understand that we can learn and apply marketing of the gospel from Jesus.[8]

In summary, marketing isn't just for corporate and technology businesses. At its essence, marketing goes beyond for-profit use. For the church, marketing is managing people's perceptions related to church products (your ministry). And it is just as important for the church to do that as it is for any company because smart marketing helps to foster church success. We purposely use the word *success*. This is a word often used in business and other organizations, where there is often the term "success criteria." In the church we have success criteria that Jesus Christ has given. Jesus tells us in John 20:21 that the Father has sent him into the world to save us from sin; he then also sends us into the world to make disciples for him. Pastors have a passion to reach their communities for Christ. We have a passion for the church to grow. We have a passion for church success. Marketing can be a tool to help.

Notes

1. Christina Hamlett, "Why Is Advertising So Important to Business?," Chron, updated February 5, 2019, http://smallbusiness.chron.com/advertising-important-business-3606.html.

2. "Definitions of Marketing," American Marketing Association, https://www.ama.org/AboutAMA/Pages/Definition-of-Marketing.aspx.

3. "The Essence of Marketing," One Sherpa, http://www.onesherpa.com/the-essence-of-marketing.html.

4. "Marketing," Harvard Business School, https://www.hbs.edu/faculty/units/marketing/Pages/default.aspx.

5. Tim Schraeder, "4 Must-Know Church Marketing Secrets," ChurchLeaders, May 9, 2019, https://churchleaders.com/worship/worship-articles/160080-4-must-know-church-marketing-secrets.html.

6. Jeremy Bradley, "Seven Functions of Marketing," Chron, updated January 25, 2019, http://smallbusiness.chron.com/seven-functions-marketing-56980.html.

7. Steve Fogg, "10 Common Branding Mistakes That Churches Make," Steve Fogg, November 21, 2012, http://www.stevefogg.com/2012/11/21/branding-churches/.

8. Jon Vaughan, "5 Insights Into Why Pastors Need a Marketing Degree," Refresh the Church, https://refreshthechurch.com/5-insights-into-why-pastors-need-a-marketing-degree/.

Resources

Books

Homan, Jason. *DIY Church Marketing*. CreateSpace, 2018.

Marshall, Greg W., and Mark W. Johnston. *Marketing Management*. 2nd Ed. New York: McGraw-Hill Education, 2014.

Reising, Richard L. *Church Marketing 101: Preparing Your Church for Greater Growth*. Grand Rapids, MI: Baker Books, 2006.

Tools

The Bantam Group. "Marketing Your Church." https://www.ng umc.org/files/fileslibrary/connectionalministries/marketing%20 your%20church.pdf.

Joubert, Devin. "30 Marketing Plan Samples and 7 Templates to Build Your Strategy." CoSchedule Blog. Updated May 28, 2018. https://coschedule.com/blog/marketing-plan-samples-and-templates/.

Weller, Joe. "Free Marketing Plan and Marketing Strategy Templates." Smartsheet. June 27, 2016. https://www.smartsheet. com/free-marketing-plan-templates-excel.

CHAPTER 9

Information Technology

Internet. Smartphones. Cloud computing. Cybersecurity. Tablets. All of these, and more, information technology tools are all around us. We live in a time when technology advances at a rapid pace. The first computer and mobile phone are nothing like the technology we have today. Further, I (Vincent) can remember the time when information technology in the church was limited to a desk telephone and a typewriter. But today, most of us would agree that the rapid advancement of information technology makes life easier and provides ministry options that were not possible before. Multimedia and internet tools have already become commonplace in many churches, and with the proliferation of smartphones and relevant software applications (apps), these tools are now a key means of communication, even in the church.

In looking at MBA programs, there is typically a course that provides students with insight into information technology management. The Illinois Institute of Technology, located in Chicago, offers a course description that provides insight into the importance of managing information technology:

> This course introduces students to the steps necessary to analyze a problem in information technology and identify and define the computing requirements appropriate to its solution, with a focus on how to design, implement, and evaluate a computer-based system, process, component, or program to meet desired needs. Students learn to analyze the local and global impact of computing on individuals,

organizations, and society. This course . . . imparts an understanding of professional, ethical, legal, security and social issues, and responsibilities in information technology. Students . . . [build] their ability to communicate effectively with a range of audiences, and work in teams learning to function effectively together to accomplish a common goal.[1]

We would contend these same reasons are relevant to the church. Is this a current fad? Because all the younger people are using apps and smartphones and other technology tools, should the greater population in the church get with the times? With more and more people and churches using personal smartphones, tablets, computers, and multimedia tools in the church, one might ask, "How should we as church leaders manage information technology for the greater benefit of the church, its ministries, and its goal of reaching others for Christ?" In spite of all its benefits, I contend that information technology should be managed strategically, and, since we live in an age of technology that impacts much of what we do, it requires careful review as to how is can best be used to build the kingdom of God. Kyle Nickel, a writer with Boxcast, which provides complete, easy-to-use live video streaming solutions for organizations, highlights from Luke 8:1-11 that as followers of Christ we are encouraged to use as many tools as possible to sow the seeds of the gospel. Nickel says:

> This passage explains the parable of the sower. Sowers do not limit themselves to certain soils; instead, they spread seeds everywhere, including rocks, thorns, or other soils thought to be less fertile. For, though uncommon, sometimes these seeds are able to flourish into something beautiful.
>
> As Christians, we are expected to do the same. We should not be selective in whom we extend ourselves to,

but rather aim to spread Christ's message to as many people as possible. Technology lets us connect with a bigger
audience than ever before.[2]

Again, the lesson for church leaders and pastors is that technology can be used to plant seeds for Christian life development
and formation.

What Is Information Technology?

Information technology (IT) is defined as "a business sector that
deals with computing, including hardware, software, telecommu-
nications and generally anything involved in the transmittal of
information or the systems that facilitate communication."[3]
Information technology management involves many facets. Take,
for instance, the IT function in a social service organization. There
are many people with many jobs—social workers, administrators,
volunteers, the executive director, and a host of other jobs with varied responsibilities. These people need to access client information,
input client records and information, prepare reports, track funding, and interface with local and state governments (including
receiving, submitting, and accessing information). As such, IT
requirements range from providing a computing system, providing
computing hardware, keeping systems and data secure, and keeping networks up and running.

There are also the decision makers, such as the IT manager (for
larger organizations, there will also be a chief information officer
[CIO]), who decide how an IT department will operate and what
computer tools and systems will be implemented and managed,
including policies and procedures. As is pointed out by
Techopedia™, a technology site that aims to provide insight and
inspiration to IT professionals, technology decision makers help
users better understand technology; information technology management "includes the management of data, whether it is in the

form of text, voice, image, audio or some other form. It can also involve things related to the Internet. This gives IT a whole new meaning, since the Internet is its own realm. IT involves the transfer of data, so it makes sense that the Internet would be a part of IT."[4] Of course, we must be mindful of the security of church members' personal information as we navigate this realm.

Church leaders, including the pastoral staff, involved in information technology management apply information technology to an organizational setting. This can be a business setting or church organization setting, including IT requirements for the facility and staff. Because the vast majority of organizations, churches included, are dependent upon some sort of computer systems to conduct business or ministry, information technology provides an important service. Some of the duties that make up the function of information technology management are included below.

■ **Website management:** Do we develop a website based on one of the free web services? Do we get better results if we hire a website developer? What are the cost considerations? Who will manage the site? Do we have internal resources to maintain the website, or will this be a recurring cost? Can we afford not to have a website? What are hosting requirements and cost?

■ **Software and application requirements:** What are our software requirements? Are there specialized packages that have benefit to the church? In addition to our website, do we need a mobile app? Who should we engage to develop the app? What is the cost of development and maintenance of the app?

■ **Hardware management:** This includes management strategies for procurement, issue, and maintenance of church IT hardware, including phone systems, printers, computers, servers, projectors, and audio/visual equipment.

■ **Database management:** A database is a data structure that stores organized information, such as tables and different fields.

For example, a church database may include tables for ministries, employees, members, visitors, and financial records. Today's databases allow users to access, input, update, and search information based on the relationship of data stored, as well as run queries that encompass multiple databases. Because these databases can contain information that should not be available to the public (e.g., records related to children involved in ministries), the function of database management becomes important. Thus, as defined by Informatica, database management refers to the actions and processes an organization employs to manipulate and control data to meet necessary conditions.[5]

■ **Device management:** Will the organization supply such items at tablets, mobile computers, and smartphones? Will employees be requested to BYOD (bring your own device)? If BYOD is applied, what guidelines should be considered regarding handling of church data (financial, members' personal data, access to church files on cloud databases)?

■ **Computer-based multimedia:** This includes hardware, software, and applications and focuses on such topics as desktop publishing, hypermedia, presentation graphics, graphic images, animation, sound, music, video, licensing, and multimedia on and from the internet.

■ **IT services:** These services include procurement sources, maintenance, repair, installation, and requirements updating.

■ **IT budgeting:** The IT function is responsible for an area that is probably second to church facility management in cost and expense. As a result, a key staff function (not the pastor) will be responsible for creating and overseeing the annual IT budget. This responsibility involves estimating and preparing the budget, approving costs and spending, reviewing contracts, and monitoring the functions (or department, depending on the size of the church) expenditures. Furthermore, this role will include meeting with the pastoral, trustee, and other upper-level church executives for budget approval.

■ **Management of technology professionals:** This area considers such topics as managing technical professionals and technology assets, human resource management, information technology budgeting and asset management, management of services, infrastructure, outsourcing, and vendor relationships, resource planning, and technology governance.

■ **Project management for IT:** For more details on church project management, see chapter 12. From an IT perspective, it is important to understand project management with a particular focus on project planning for information technology hardware, software, networking, church app development, website development and project implementation, and building and leading effective teams.

■ **Data security:** Church leaders need to engage in an in-depth examination of topics related to data security, including security considerations related to members' personal information, church financial information, background check information, encryption methods, cryptography law, and church computer system security architecture and models.

■ **Cybersecurity:** This function includes management of IT challenges such as viruses, worms, and other attack mechanisms, vulnerabilities, and their related countermeasures. This function comprises network security protocols, encryption, identity and authentication, firewalls, and security tools, in order for the organization to address IT security so that there is operations and system continuity.

■ **Data analytics:** This area focuses on the creation, maintenance, analysis, and modeling of relevant church data that will help the church improve its ministry performance. For example, churches would benefit from creating a database (or buying a software tool or getting a volunteer with this expertise) that tracks not only attendance but also visitor information, attendance at events, member participation, first-time visitor repeat attendance, and other information, in order to gather statistical data to determine improvement opportunities. For example, what does the data say about frequency of returning visitors, and how can we make improvements to this data point? Data analytics supports decision making; see also chapter 5 on decision making.

■ **IT auditing:** The process of IT auditing centers on verifying that the organization is performing to requirements and standards. An audit can apply to an entire organization or might be specific to a function or process, such as reliability and performance of computers and multimedia equipment or proper use of church-issued computers and smartphones. Standard practices and standards in the auditing of information technology are required. In IT terminology, the typical audit includes IT governance, systems and infrastructure life cycle management, IT service delivery and support, protection of information assets, organizational continuity, and disaster recovery.

■ **Consulting with technical professionals:** Pastors or other church leaders would benefit from developing skills in working with business, industry, or various professions who assist churches in solving specific IT problems (consultants and solution providers). Considerations include involving appropriate parties in all phases of problem identification and solution with the goal that, at the end of a consulting assignment, the church is able to sustain the solution, including the necessary changes required in the organization (managing expectations among change agents, church leaders, staff, church technical professionals, and other members of the organization).

Information Technology and the Church Today

As you, the readers, have likely gathered from the above discussion and from your experience, churches use many types of information and computer technology. Search the topic online and you will discover that new technologies are being made available to users all the time. Technology is rapidly changing. So your church's strategy and tactics for managing its information technology are critical. In my study of the topic, along with Scripture and my ministry experience, I am led to believe that information technology is a resource that we as a church can use for God's glory and to bring others to Christ. Here are several key points that church research has documented.

First, as pointed out by Ed Stetzer in *Christianity Today*, technology enables communication:

> Through Facebook and Twitter or through a church blog, I can easily communicate directly with the people in my congregation, throughout the day and week.
>
> For example, I have a full-time job with LifeWay, so I am able to pastor a church by preaching, meeting with the staff, and leading a small group in my home.
>
> That's all I can physically do. But I can pastor my church all throughout the week through social media and digital technology.
>
> Technology enables the congregation easily to have direct communication with me, and I can have communication with them on a broader and a clearer scale.
>
> Ongoing communication through technology helps the mission of the church. In fact, as I told Leadership Journal only half-jokingly, pastors who aren't on Twitter need to repent.[6]

Second, a team of consultants at Church Tech Today contends that church information technology can "play a key role in helping your church identify, improve, and activate an assimilation process that grows your church by effectively integrating first-time guests." The article presents two key observations:

■ Technology helps the church define its first-time guest process. "It only takes seven minutes for a guest to formulate a first impression of your church. Technology helps you define your church's first-time guest process by helping you evaluate when they are being greeted and how they are being greeted."

■ Technology helps to improve the way a church follows up and follows through with guests. "You can record a first-time guest's personal communication preferences and follow up in a way that's most appealing to them. Technology also allows you to assign contacts for initial follow-up and track activity through the assimilation process so no one falls through the cracks."[7]

Last, as followers of Jesus Christ, we are called to go and make disciples, as we are taught in Matthew 28:19. We are called to reach out to people—all people, all cultures, all races, everywhere. Sometimes this means going door-to-door. At other times it means getting out into the community. At other times, the Lord requires us to be creative with the talents and blessings bestowed on us to reach those outside the church or those who are hurting. Dale B. Sims, in an article posted on the Dallas Baptist University website, contends that technology can be a tool to spread the gospel. He gives an insightful example in "The Effect of Technology on Christianity: Blessing or Curse?":

> In the U.S. today there are over 800 megachurches. These are churches that regularly have over 2000 people attending services. It is predicted that one church, First Baptist of Houston, will soon have over 35,000 worshippers every Sunday. Some churches in South Korea have reported over 250,000 attendees every Sunday. The Potter's House, right next door to DBU, can accommodate almost 12,000 people every Sunday. Within the sanctuary 200 pews provide power and data terminals so worshippers can download sermon notes, PowerPoint presentations, and Bible passages. [Altar]

attendants armed with [handheld devices] collect prayer needs and new-member data to download into the church server. The sermon is translated via wireless headphones into one of six languages. None of the above would be possible without supporting technologies.[8]

So, information technology is a valuable tool for enabling ministry productivity. Its implementation should not be trivial but strategic.

Tools for Managing Church Information Technology

We live in a continuously and rapidly changing world, in and outside of the church, of information technology. Change has affected not only organizations but also the personal lives of church members. For example, many churches no longer depend on giving via the offering plate; online giving is becoming the norm. Members no longer need to write checks; they can schedule their giving through online banking. So, what IT tools can the church utilize as it seeks to fulfill the Great Commission and minister effectively to the congregation and community? Below is a sampling of tools that are available. It is not intended to be exhaustive; the breadth of what is available likely could comprise a book. Our recommendation is to do an online search on the topics shown.

- Church management software
- Information technology auditing tools
- Church website development
- Church app development
- Free project management software
- Church cybersecurity
- Email marketing
- Free video conferencing
- IT management tools

- Church presentation software
- IT audit checklist

We have included a resource list at the end of the chapter. Please take a look to find additional information, including website links and book and article recommendations. And for church information technology management, there is an online forum for church technology leaders that is a good resource for information and for getting input on specific technologies or applications. The organization is called Church Technical Leaders, and it's a site built around ministry using technology. The group describes itself:

> Church Technical Leaders continues to be a resource led by full-time church technical leaders, pursuing the mission of fostering relationships among members; equipping leaders by facilitating peer learning, and encouraging synergy through the sharing of ideas. "Our ministry is wrapping our arms around serving the local church through the technical arts. This is the beginning of a new journey and we look forward to seeing what God has in store!"[9]

Ron Sellers, president of Ellison Research in Phoenix, Arizona, which has been serving the Christian community through research since 1987, provides an appropriate summary on the importance of information technology management for the church:

> Technology by itself is also not relevant. There must be a reason to use it, a strategy for its use, the ability to use it well, someone to oversee it use, and a way to measure whether it is having the desired impact. Without these elements in place, it's just one more thing draining much-needed resources or causing a distraction. With these elements in place, technology can have a significant and positive effect on ministry.[10]

Notes

1. "Information Technology and Management," Illinois Institute of Technology, https://appliedtech.iit.edu/information-technology-and-management/course-descriptions.

2. Kyle Nickel, "4 Bible Verses That Encourage Technology in Ministry," Boxcast, March 6, 2019, https://www.boxcast.com/blog/4-bible-verses-that-encourage-technology-in-ministry.

3. "Information Technology (IT)" Techopedia, https://www.tech opedia.com/definition/626/information-technology-it.

4. Ibid.

5. Informatica, https://www.informatica.com/about-us/why-informatica.html. Informatica is a premier organization that helps organizations overcome market disruptions, grow, and thrive by fueling data innovation.

6. Ed Stetzer, "3 Ways Technology Enables the Mission of the Church," Christianity Today, October 27, 2014, https://www.christianitytoday.com/edstetzer/2014/october/3-ways-technology-enables-mission-of-church.html.

7. "5 Ways Technology Accelerates Church Growth," Church Tech Today, September 11, 2013, https://churchtechtoday.com/2013/09/11/5-ways-technology-accelerates-church-growth/.

8. Dale B. Sims, "The Effect of Technology on Christianity: Blessing or Curse?," Dallas Baptist University, 7, https://www3.dbu.edu/Naugle/pdf/The%20Effect%20of%20Technology%20o n%20Christianity2.pdf.

9. "The Purpose and Vision of Church Tech Leaders," Church Production, https://www.churchproduction.com/education/the-purpose-and-vision-of-church-tech-leaders/.

10. Ron Sellers, "Technology and Ministry Current Trends," *The Clergy Journal*, January 2007, 12, https://greymatter research.com/index_files/Grey_Matter_Article_Ministry_Technolo gy.pdf.

Resources

Books

Cox, Brandon. *Rewired: How Using Today's Technology Can Bring You Back to Deeper Relationships, Real Conversations, and the Age-Old Methods of Sharing God's Love.* Lake Mary, FL: Charisma House, 2014.

Petrozzo, Daniel P. *The Fast Forward MBA in Technology Management.* Hoboken, NJ: John Wiley & Sons, 1998.

Wise, Justin. *The Social Church: A Theology of Digital Communication.* Chicago: Moody Publishers, 2014.

Tools

Chang, Jenny. "21 Best Church Management Software Solutions of 2019." Finances Online. https://financesonline.com/top-20-church-management-software-solutions/.

Detwiler, Bill. "100+ IT policies at your fingertips, ready to download," ZDNet. July 22, 2019. https://www.zdnet.com/article/100-it-policies-at-your-fingertips-ready-for-download/.

CHAPTER 10

Strategic Planning

Noted leadership guru Peter Drucker once said, "Plans are only good intentions unless they immediately degenerate into hard work."[1] In order for any organization—church, nonprofit, or manufacturing company—to achieve its objectives, planning, and in particular strategic planning, is required. Successful organizational planning needs objectives to be set and strategies to be created, implemented, and measured. This chapter will help you think about the importance of applying the strategic planning process. Our intent is to use strategic thinking to help you develop a sound understanding of the ministry opportunities and challenges facing your congregation in its ministry context. In particular, considerations in this chapter include an introduction to strategic planning, a discussion of objectives, external and internal analysis, and strategy implementation, which includes action planning, implementation (projects), and evaluation of strategy performance. As a starting point, strategic planning is our road map for achieving the mission statement or objectives of your local church.

What Does the Bible Say about Strategic Planning?
Many have heard the old saying that is often attributed to Benjamin Franklin: "If you fail to plan, you are planning to fail." Granted, this quote can be considered worldly, so let's look at the Word to get insight on the theological foundation for strategic planning. Several Scriptures speak to strategic planning. Here is a sample:

Commit your work to the LORD, and your plans will be established (Proverbs 16:3, ESV).

> For I know the plans I have for you, declares the LORD, plans for welfare and not for evil, to give you a future and a hope (Jeremiah 29:11, ESV).

> Do not be conformed to this world, but be transformed by the renewal of your mind, that by testing you may discern what is the will of God, what is good and acceptable and perfect (Romans 12:2, ESV).

> The plans of the diligent lead surely to abundance, but everyone who is hasty comes only to poverty (Proverbs 21:5, ESV).

Each of these verses speaks to the importance of purposely planning the work the Lord has committed to us as leaders in the church. Planning our work as leaders requires committing our work to the Lord, listening to the lead of the Holy Spirt and not to the world as we plan, being diligent in that work, and having a confidence that as we follow the Lord, God will prosper our work.

Mark Marshall, regional manager with LifeWay Church Resources in Nashville, Tennessee, shares another theological view of strategic planning from Scripture:

> Joshua, the protégé of Moses, also demonstrated strategic leadership. In Joshua 6, God gave Joshua a little lesson on strategic thinking. As Joshua was to lead the Israelites into the Promised Land, they were facing the first enemy in the land. It just so happened to be the strong city of Jericho. God gave Joshua a strategy. He could have simply reached down from heaven and zapped the city, but God chose to work through a strategy that involved His people. God continues to work through His people today.[2]

God clearly expects us as pastors to plan. Strategic planning is one of several tools the Lord provides that helps us to achieve the short- and long-term objectives God has put on our hearts as leaders in local congregations. With the many Scriptures God gave us, it is imperative that we trust the Lord's direction and not our own plans and tactics. As Marshall emphasizes, "It is only after we seek the heart of God and His direction that we can establish plans that are pleasing to Him and plans that will succeed."[3]

What Is Strategic Planning?

Strategic planning is used in many different types of organizations. This includes large corporations, governments (local, state, and federal), nonprofits, and churches. The goal of any organization's strategic plan is to identify what an organization is trying to do and then lay out a plan to use accessible resources to achieve these aims. I (Vincent) use the word *accessible* in order to emphasize that a local church's resources are not limited to just those resources that are available in the local church. There are other accessible resources in the broader community. So, let's start with a definition of strategic management. When I taught the topic in a graduate school course, the definition I favored was as follows:

> Strategic management is a set of managerial decisions and actions that determines the long-run performance of a corpo-ration. It includes environmental scanning (both external and internal) strategy formulation, (strategic or long-range plan-ning) strategy implementation, and evaluation and control. The study of strategic management, therefore, emphasizes the monitoring and evaluating of external opportunities and threats in light of a corporation's strengths and weaknesses.[4]

Strategic planning helps an organization. The Balanced Scorecard Institute (BSI), a strategy management company in Cary,

North Carolina, highlights some important insights about strategic planning:

> Strategic planning is an organizational management activity that is used to set priorities, focus energy and resources, strengthen operations, ensure that employees and other stakeholders are working toward common goals, establish agreement around intended outcomes/results, and assess and adjust the organization's direction in response to a changing environment. It is a disciplined effort that produces fundamental decisions and actions that shape and guide what an organization is, who it serves, what it does, and why it does it, with a focus on the future. Effective strategic planning articulates not only where an organization is going and the actions needed to make progress, but also how it will know if it is successful.[5]

The BSI summary includes some important needs that impact the church. For example, churches, especially small and medium-sized churches, are often challenged with limited resources, few employees, and, at times, turnover of volunteers in ministries. There is a dedicated group of members who will often commit unlimited time and resources in an attempt to help get church work done. However, we can get caught up in doing church work instead of the work of the church—making disciples for Christ, transforming communities and the lives of neighbors—that we continue to do what we have always done, never stopping to consider or evaluate the effectiveness of our efforts. So, when we as pastors work alongside the laity to think about and execute the work of the Lord strategically, we are able to see that strategic planning will help us set priorities, focus energy, more effectively manage resources, develop more effective operations, and ensure that everyone in the church—members, volunteers, and employees—works toward shared goals and gains consensus around intended objectives and their resulting outcomes. Finally, a strategic plan that the church is executing also gives the church the opportunity to evaluate and adjust its direction in response to outcomes and any changes happening in the church or community it serves (this is often referred to as the environment).

Len Moisan, founder and president of The Covenant Group, highlights six benefits of using a church strategic planning process:

1. Clarifies mission and core values
2. Identifies priorities
3. Establishes clear direction
4. Focuses decision making
5. Enhances communication and teamwork
6. Increases success[6]

The strategic planning process can be a valuable experience for your church leaders. Planning helps any church navigate the changing social landscape it now operates in. There is good evidence that, with strategic thinking, churches are better able to adapt in a world where the numbers of churchgoers are declining. Strategic planning may be a good solution to address the future.

How to Do Strategic Planning

In view of the benefits highlighted above, let's look at how to do strategic management, that is, to prepare a strategic plan. In making a strategic plan, it is important to have a model or template. In this section, I will present a model that I feel will be useful for churches. By having a guideline, it is my desire to provide a how-to or what-to-do perspective. But before we look at this model, I want to emphasize that doing strategic planning is not just a leadership tool. It is a spiritual focus tool. Just as prayer and Bible study are critical in planning any ministry, such is the case for strategic management and planning. The leader must approach the task as a spiritual discipline. Stephen A. Macchia, founding president of Leadership Transformations, a ministry focusing on spiritual formation of leaders and the spiritual discernment of leadership, emphasizes this point by noting seven things pastors should avoid as they approach strategic planning.

- Making planning too complex
- Not reaching conclusions and making an action plan
- Not keeping the action plan simple
- Not revisiting the plan
- Taking too long
- Trusting your instincts apart from prayer[7]

Macchia's last point is especially   important. Praying before and during the planning process is essential. As the apostle Paul reminds us, "I urge, then, first of all, that petitions, prayers, intercession and thanksgiving be made for all people" (1 Timothy 2:1, NIV). During your strategic planning process, emphasize to your team and the entire congregation that it is impossible to do the work God is calling us to without the means of prayer to which God calls us. I urge you to intercede for all those involved in the planning process (staff, pastors, ministry volunteers, community resources, etc.). Pray for a spirit of oneness, wisdom, insight, the Lord's direction, prudence, clarity, vision, and the leadership of the Holy Spirit.

A Model for Strategic Planning

As I mentioned above, I taught strategic planning at the graduate school at Elmira College. I was teaching as part of the Master of Science in Management program. Most of the students were focusing on careers in business, healthcare, or not-for-profit organization leadership. The strategic planning framework I taught was developed by the late Thomas L. Wheelen, DBA, and a professor of strategic management at the University of South Florida, and his colleague, Dr. J. David Hunger. Keys to their strategic management framework were four concepts:

- Environmental scanning
- Strategy formulation
- Strategy implementation
- Evaluation and control

Following are definitions for each component.

Environmental scanning "is a process that systematically surveys and interprets relevant data to identify external opportunities and threats. An organization gathers information about the external world, its competitors and itself. The company should then respond to the information gathered by changing its strategies and plans when the need arises."[8]

Strategy formulation is "the process of choosing the most appropriate course of action for the realization of organizational goals and objectives and thereby achieving the organizational vision."[9]

Strategy implementation "is a process that puts plans and strategies into action to reach desired goals. The strategic plan itself is a written document that details the steps and processes needed to reach plan goals, and includes feedback and progress reports to ensure that the plan is on track."[10]

The function of evaluation and control is to determine performance to plan. It might be considered a performance appraisal. From the church's perspective, it helps us to give objective feedback so that improvements can be made as we progress toward success in meeting goals and objectives. Aubrey Malphurs, a professor of pastoral ministries at Dallas Theological Seminary, highlights that there are six purposes of evaluation and control: 1) evaluation accomplishes ministry alignment, 2) evaluation prioritizes ministry accomplishment, 3) evaluation encourages ministry assessment, 4) evaluation coaxes ministry affirmation, 5) evaluation emboldens ministry correction, and 6) evaluation elicits ministry improvement.[11] And as Wheelen and Hunger assert, "Evaluation and control processes ensure that an [organization] is achieving what it set out to accomplish. It compares performance with desired results and provides feedback necessary for management to evaluate results and take corrective action, as needed."[12] Evaluation and control, which closes the loop that started with planning, is achieved using this five-step feedback model:

Determine what to measure
Establish standards of performance
Measure actual performance
Compare actual performance with the standard
Take corrective action[13]

Figure 10.1 provides a graphic representation of the above components of strategic planning. As you can see from the figure, this model provides a disciplined and methodical approach to strategic management and planning. As a pastor, when teaching the course to students in a graduate school, I concluded that, though it was not specifically a model focused on the church as an organization, it adapts well for use in the church.

**Figure 10.1. Summary of the Wheelen and Hunger
Strategic Management Model**

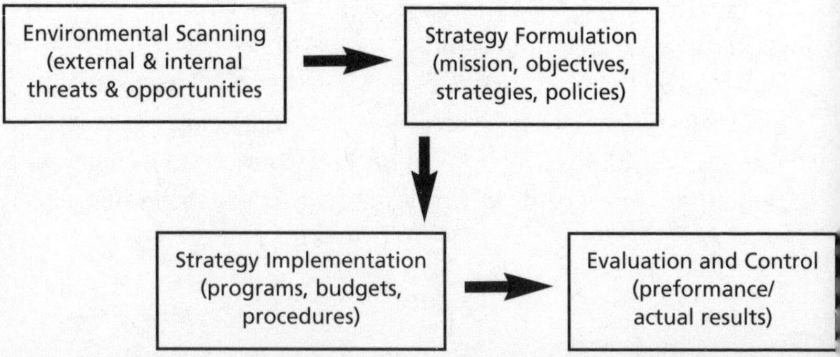

To apply this model in a church context, I would make adaptations based on Scripture's guidance for leadership. For example, in the church all critical decisions should start with the discernment of where God is leading. Scripture is specific on this. Proverbs 3:6 (KJV) informs us, "In all thy ways acknowledge him, and he shall direct thy paths." In order to acknowledge God's leading, we must seek direction from Scripture and through prayer. The advice the Lord gives us in 1 John 5:14 (NIV) is that "this is the confidence we have in approaching God: that if we ask anything according to his will, he hears us." So, prayer must cover the beginning and each step of the process. In this regard, I would add a column before Environmental Scanning titled Prayer and Mission Reflection and a bar titled Prayer at the top of the figure that covers each of the phases to indicate that prayer should continue with each phase.

Another consideration for the church and this model is how we approach the Environmental Scanning phase. What I mean by this is that from a church perspective, the environmental scanning needs to address opportunities and threats regarding things like neighborhood needs, community needs, church situation, and society trends, instead of industry analysis. Furthermore, we also need think about where God is calling us—congregational expectations and church resources (gifts, skills, and knowledge). With these considerations, I would visualize this model from a church perspective as shown in Figure 10.2.

**Figure 10.2. Church Considerations for Applying the
Wheelen and Hunger Model**

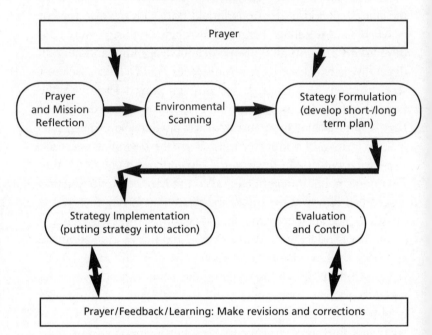

With this adaptation of the Wheelen and Hunger model, initial prayer is critical—prayer by leaders and the congregation as the leadership teams prepare to undertake the strategic planning exercise. Furthermore, at the start of the planning phase, again prayer must be the starting point by the leadership team as it proceeds with mission reflection. Our foundational Scripture for strategic planning should be based on our mission to go and make disciples for Jesus Christ (Matthew 28:19).

In closing this chapter, it is important to note that church leaders must be creative and strategic in thought and action. New ministry strategies are required in all church settings as we continuously adapt to the changing world we live in. Reaching others so that they believe in the Lord Jesus Christ is what we are called to do. To do this, the leadership team must be strategic. Thomas G. Bandy, an internationally recognized church consultant and leadership coach who works across the spectrum of church traditions, makes an important point that is a critical reminder as we close this chapter:

> The most remarkable thing about strategic thinking is that it changes the character of the church. The church is no longer an institution on its own but only one player in the Christian movement. Strategic thinking isn't really about producing better programs, deploying better personnel, maintaining sacred space, raising more money, or even solving social problems. It's really about sustaining a movement that generates more leaders who generate more leaders, or in more spiritual terminology, a succession of servants who mentor more servants. It's not what you do but how you think.[14]

Notes

1. "Peter Drucker Quotes about Planning," AZ Quotes, https://www.azquotes.com/author/4147-Peter_Drucker/tag/planning.

2. Mark Marshall, "Is Strategic Planning Biblical?," Christianity Today, July 12, 2007, https://www.christianitytoday.com/pastors/2007/july-online-only/le-031112a.html.

3. Ibid.

4. Thomas L. Wheelen and J. David Hunger, *Strategic Management and Business Policy: Toward Global Sustainability*, 13th ed. (Upper Saddle River, NJ: Pearson Education Foundation, 2012), 5.

5. "Strategic Planning Basics," Strategy Management Group, http://www.balancedscorecard.org/BSC-Basics/Strategic-Planning-Basics. The Balanced Scorecard Institute provides consulting, training, and professional certification services to commercial, government, and nonprofit organizations globally.

6. Len Moisan, "How Your Church Benefits from Strategic Planning," The Covenant Group, June 2, 2016, https://covenant grouponline.com/2016/06/how-your-church-benefits-from-strate gic-planning/. The Covenant Group, based in Louisville, Kentucky, is a consulting organization that helps churches and nonprofit organizations reach their growth and funding goals through an array of services and products related to church strategic planning and leadership development.

7. Stephen A. Macchia, "Do's and Don'ts in Developing a Strategy," Christianity Today, https://www.christianitytoday.com/pastors/2007/july-online-only/070204a.html.

8. "Strategic Planning: What Are the Basics of Environmental Scanning?," SHRM, November 27, 2012, https://www.shrm.org/resourcesandtools/tools-and-samples/hr-qa/pages/basics-of-envi ronmental-scanning.aspx.

9. Prachi Juneja, "Steps in Strategy Formulation Process," Management Study Guide, https://www.managementstudyguide.com/strategy-formulation-process.htm.

10. Kristie Lorette, "What Is Strategic Implementation?," Chron, June 30, 2018, https://smallbusiness.chron.com/strategic-imple mentation-5044.html.

11. Aubrey Malphurs, *Advanced Strategic Management: A New Model for Church and Ministry Leaders* (Grand Rapids, MI: Baker Books, 1999), 202–4.

12. Wheelen and Hunger, *Strategic Management and Business Policy*, 328.

13. Ibid., 328, 330.

14. Thomas G. Bandy, *Strategic Thinking: How to Sustain Effective Ministry* (Nashville: Abingdon, 2017), 189–90.

Resources
Books
Bandy, Thomas G. *Strategic Thinking: How to Sustain Effective Ministry.* Nashville: Abingdon, 2017.

Malphurs, Aubrey. *Advanced Strategic Management: A New Model for Church and Ministry Leaders.* Grand Rapids, MI: Baker Books, 1999.

Articles
Buer, Aaron. "4 Questions that Guide Our Church's Strategic Plan." Breeze. January 25, 2018. https://www.breezechms.com/blog/4-questions-that-guide-our-churchs-strategic-plan/.

Macchia, Stephen A. "Do's and Don'ts in Developing a Strategy." Christianity Today. https://www.christianitytoday.com/pastors-/2007/july-online-only/070204a.html.

Tools
Breeze Church Software. https://www.breezechms.com/.

Jurevicius, Ovidijus. "SWOT Analysis – Do It Properly!" Strategic Management Insight. February 13, 2013. https://www.strategicmanagementinsight.com/tools/swot-analysis-how-to-do-it.html.

Lotich, Patricia. "5 Easy Steps to Writing a Church Mission, Vision and Values Statement." Smart Church Management. April 18, 2018. https://smartchurchmanagement.com/church-vision-mission-and-values-statement/.

Rainer, Thom S. "How to Develop a Church Mission/Vision Statement. Revitalized Churches. http://revitalizedchurches.com/wp-content/uploads/2014/11/How-to-Develop-a-Church-Vision-Statement.pdf.

CHAPTER 11

Innovation

When we think of innovation, the church is usually not at the forefront of our thinking. When it comes to innovation, new tech products, new businesses out of Silicon Valley, a university-based think tank, that new business that just opened in our neighborhood, or the research university that helps spur new startups come to mind more frequently. Innovation as a foundation in the church—not so much!

Yet I contend that innovation has a place in the church. Romans 12:2 (NIV) is a good starting point: "Do not conform to the pattern of this world, but be transformed by the renewing of your mind. Then you will be able to test and approve what God's will is—his good, pleasing and perfect will." Melinda Emerson, author, speaker, Christian, small business coach, and CEO of Quintessence Multimedia, comments that "the bible commands us to be innovative in our businesses. We should not ever try to be like anyone else. The world is still waiting on a better mousetrap, and we should never rest on our successes. We must renew ourselves by being lifelong learners and reading constantly."[1]

This chapter is designed to share insight into the concept of innovation and innovation thinking. We will look at current theory on innovation thinking, along with implications for the church. In addition, we will seek to provide an innovation process that can be applied in current church environments. The current state of the church and changing demographics require that innovation become a leading tool for developing growth and evangelistic ministries. Innovation has long been considered a competency of technology, new business startups (entrepreneurship), and engineering, but that has become insufficient today. Churches and church organizations need innovation to develop community and demographic-specific solutions to achieve the objective of making disciples for Christ for the transformation of the world.

A Definition of Innovation

Let's start with a working definition of innovation. As Scott Anthony, author of *The Little Black Book of Innovation* notes, "a simple, five-word definition [of innovation is] 'Something different that has impact.'" Anthony further states that "innovation is a process that combines discovering an opportunity, blueprinting an idea to seize that opportunity, and implementing that idea to achieve results. Remember—no impact, no innovation."[2] So, when we start to understand this concept, innovation is about positive change, shifting, revolution, disruption of the status quo, transformation, metamorphosis, breakthrough. It is about new things or new ways of doing things that have an impact.

One point that we want to make before moving on to discuss why innovation is important in the church is why innovation is important to any organization. Cleverism, an organization that focuses on insightful, practical advice and actionable tools for leaders, highlights several benefits to having an innovation strategy:[3]

- Solving problems
- Adapting to change
- Maximizing on diversity
- Facing up to the competition
- Evolving workplace dynamics
- Customers' changing tastes and preferences

Why Innovation Is Important in the Church

If we affirm that innovation is a process that combines discovering an opportunity for ministry, blueprinting and designing strategies for executing an idea to seize that opportunity, and implementing that ministry idea to achieve life-changing, kingdom-glorifying results (remember: no impact, no innovation), then innovation in the church is paramount. A recent United Methodist Church study went so far as to say in the denomination's Call to Action Steering Team that "business as usual is unsustainable. Instead, dramatically different new behaviors, not incremental changes, are required."[4] And more broadly, Deborah Bruce, project director for the US Congregational Life Survey, determined the importance of innovation to church growth, concluding, "Just doing what we've always done is not going to necessarily work in today's culture."[5]

It goes without saying that, as it relates to pastoral leadership in today's new reality of cultural, technological, and spiritual change, church leaders must apply innovation to ministry and leadership. It will not be acceptable to lead as if we live in a world like that of fifty years ago. Larry Osborne, a senior pastor at North Coast Church in Vista, California, and author of *Sticky Leaders: The Secret to Lasting Change and Innovation*, makes a relevant point in this regard:

> Change and innovation are a necessary part of creating the future. Without the organizational agility to make necessary changes, your church will soon die and God will have to raise up wildfire down the street (and trust me, he will). At the end of the day, change is a lot like electricity. Handled well, it brings great blessings. Handled carelessly or without understanding, it can burn the house down.[6]

As you might expect, there are a number of trends affecting today's church. With my background of being a bi-vocational pastor and a student of leadership, I am sensitive to broad leadership lessons and how they might apply to the church. Brian Dodd seems to have a similar outlook of applying leadership lessons. Dodd is the author and content coordinator for a website called Brian Dodd on Leadership, and he is Director of New Ministry Partnerships for INJOY Stewardship Solutions, where he helps churches develop cultures of generosity. He found an article in *Fast Company* that identified lessons about innovation from highly effective and successful organizations. From this, he created a list of how these lessons apply to the church, including the concept of innovation.[7]

1. Inspiration needs execution: There is no creativity without creation… Creatives must actually create something.

2. Tomorrow is too slow: Church staff historically do not follow up with people and on projects well. This is something which [we as church workers] must improve.

3. Great ideas need time: Do not minimize the power of prayer. Ideas need time to mature. Think about it, food simply tastes better coming out of a crockpot rather than a microwave.

4. Innovative cultures are rewarding: Churches who constantly innovate and introduce new things often experience high levels of growth and momentum.

5. Innovation can generate revenue: Churches who innovate can often better connect people's heart to the heart of God. Frequently, a result of this deepened relationship is an increased flow in financial resources into the Kingdom.

6. Millennials matter: Young people can bring new vision and fresh energy for how they work into your church.

7. Ability to scale: Innovative churches (and most other churches as well) have discovered multi-site, video venues, and re-launches of dying churches is the best way to scale ministry.

8. Innovation works best in collaboration: You can simply accomplish more with a team than you can alone.

9. Platforms are powerful: Apps, interactive websites, and constant e-communications allow people to be impacted by your ministry seven days a week.

10. Data driven: Statistics tell us about trends. They also tell us about our people. Every number has a name. Every name has a story. Every story matters to God.

11. The importance of technology: The most important component of churches who exceed budget is digital giving. Digital giving prevents summer slumps, allows people to go on vacations, and prevents [against the effects of] inclement weather.

12. Make your church an experience: In addition to food courts, new shopping malls are offering fashion shows, gaming areas, internet work stations, virtual tours, and central areas for online ordering as part of the everyday experience. What's in your lobby? What's in your hallways?

13. Design is important: How your services and ministries look and feel are determining factors in whether visitors will return to your church or not. Design tells visitors, "We were expecting you."

14. New ideas are constantly originating: Because we have the Creator living in and through us, Christians should be the most innovative people in the world. And local churches should be the most innovative place in your community.

15. Teamwork is still important: It makes the dream work.

16. Innovation should be easy to experience: Never innovate for the sake of innovation. Always innovate for the purpose of making it easier for those in your church to connect to the heart of God.[8]

For pastors and church leaders, innovation is an important part of your leadership strategy. Being an innovative, vital, and fruitful church is more than just growth in membership and attendance numbers. At the foundation of any church, large or small, are relationships with God, relationships with people who are being served in the community, and relationships with current and future disciples. Innovation in ministries, service, outreach, and leadership is critical to serving the present age.

Understanding Innovation Models and Application in the Church

As a pastor, I hope you are asking, Does innovation relate to me? Do all churches need to be innovative? Is there a process that can be used to come up with an innovation? The answer is yes, yes, and yes!

I recall the days when I was working as an engineering manager and pastoring a medium-sized church. The company that I worked for had a strong emphasis on new product and process innovation. More strategically, it had an organizational framework and commitment to achieve its goals by doing what it did best—transforming industries, enhancing people's lives, and delivering disruptive innovations that created value for decades. In other words, the organization was always thinking long-term, even to the extent of being innovative in reinventing the company and product/technology line in order to stay relevant for the long haul. It approached innovation strategically.

But innovation is not easy or a simple process. Innovation is more than coming up with new ideas. It takes more than that. Innovation experts tend to agree that a successful innovation process must insist that innovation be managed not by individual idea generators or small teams or auxiliaries working in silos, asking for support from the organization or working independently, but by multidisciplinary groups throughout the organization.[9] Gary P. Pisano, an innovation expert, professor of Business Administration, and member of the U.S. Competitiveness Project at Harvard Business School, reinforces the criticality of approaching innovation as strategic for any organization, including the church:

> The problem with innovation improvement efforts is rooted in the lack of an *innovation strategy*.
>
> A strategy is nothing more than a commitment to a set of coherent, mutually reinforcing policies or behaviors aimed at achieving a specific competitive goal. Good

strategies promote alignment among diverse groups within an organization, clarify objectives and priorities, and help focus efforts around them.[10]

So, for the church to implement innovation strategically, it must be part of the way it operates. It must be in the organization's DNA. This includes having a methodology or organizational model for how it will not only encourage innovation but also evaluate ideas from inception through implementation. Some organizations will refer to this model as a "stage gate process."

There are numerous models that are likely discussed in an MBA course. An internet search will result in a number of graphic illustrations of innovations processes that various organizations use. Examples of this include the Corning Innovation Model, described in a Massachusetts Institute of Technology case study prepared by Rebecca M. Henderson and Cate Reavis.[11] The DeSai Group, a consultancy that has served domestic and international businesses and industries in responding to changing business, economic climates, new challenges, and competition, has a model described as the Innovation Funnel.[12] Both of these models are worth studying to gain greater knowledge about formal innovation process implementation. To give a more detailed insight into how an innovation model might work, I will discuss the Tucker model of innovation.

The Tucker model of innovation was developed by Robert M. Tucker, who is president of The Innovation Resource, a Christian, and the author of the international bestseller *Managing the Future*. On innovation, Robert Tucker's position is that:

> innovation will become a required operational discipline. Managing innovation in this environment involves four key principles: the approach must be comprehensive; innovation must include an organized, systematic, and continual search for new opportunities; organizations

must involve everyone in the innovation process; [and an organization] must work constantly on improving its climate for innovation.[13]

With this foundation, the Tucker model emphasizes that the innovation process must be approached from a systematic perspective. Figure 11.1 shows the Tucker model of innovation.

Figure 11.1. Tucker Innovation Model

TUCKER INNOVATION MODEL

FILLING THE IDEA FUNNEL →

IDEA GENERATION METHODS | IDEA MANAGEMENT SYSTEMS | CUSTOMER INSIGHT METHODS | OPEN INNOVATION SYSTEMS | FUTURE MINING TECHNIQUES | DISRUPTION OPPORTUNITY ANALYSIS

INNOVATION RESULTS MANAGEMENT
BUILD CUSTOMER ACCEPTANCE
EVALUATE RESULTS

PROTOTYPING
RESEARCH & REFINEMENT
PILOT TEST
The THROUGHPUT DEVELOPMENT CYCLE
(PRODUCT / SERVICE / PROCESS / STRATEGY INNOVATION)
BUSINESS CASE
Idea
PILOT LAUNCH
Factory
IDEA SELECTION PROCESS
RAPID PROTOTYPE
LAUNCH

No Go | Go

Inputs | **Throughputs** | **Outputs**

8 BUILDING BLOCKS OF INNOVATION | INNOVATION STRATEGY & DEFINITION | LEADING & CHAMPIONNING INNOVATION | RESOURCE ALLOCATION | DEVELOPING INNOVATION SKILLS | MANAGEMENT REWARDS & METRICS | CULTIVATING THE CULTURE | INVOLVING THE WHOLE ENTERPRISE | COLLABORATING WITH CUSTOMERS & STAKEHOLDERS

©2016 by Innovation Resource Consulting Group and ITD Group

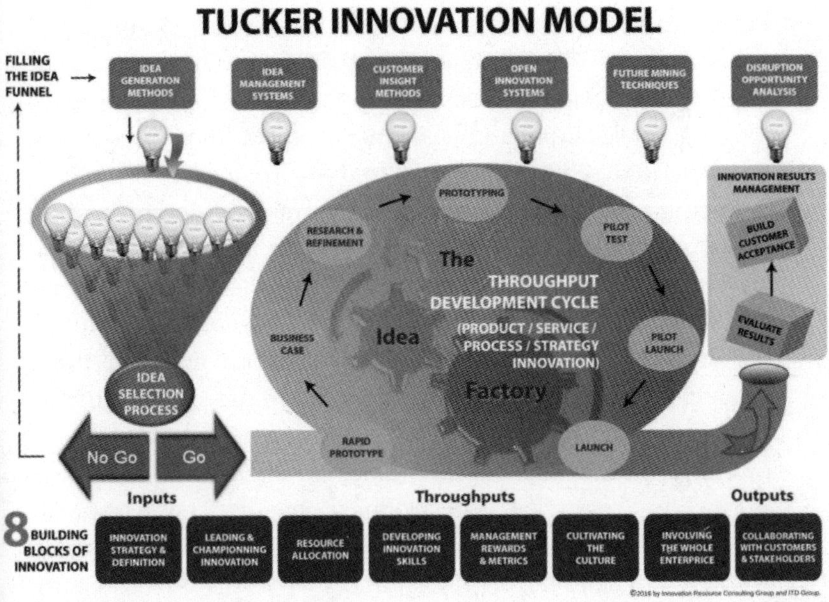

Source: Robert B. Tucker. Used with permission.

The model has a foundation of eight building blocks: innovation strategy and definition, leading and championing innovation, resource allocation, developing innovation skills within the organization, management rewards and metrics, cultivating the innovation culture within the organization, involving the whole enterprise (organization), and collaboration with customers and others who have a vested interest (stakeholders). These building blocks support the critical components of people, organization, and process.

With the building blocks in place, the organization (rather than a single idea generator) works to generate ideas that result in new or innovative products, services, ministries, methods, or processes. This idea generation process is supported by management systems, customer insight, open innovation systems, mining (idea mining is a research strategy that aims to extend the benefits of information retrieval from vast databases of information so proposed ideas can be extracted), and disruptive opportunity analysis. A disruptive opportunity is how an organization can positively respond and benefit from context changes (e.g., the newspaper industry's response to digital publishing and the internet). In the church this might mean the church's response to digital technology.

After ideas are generated, there is a formal decision process to decide which the organization will focus on (a go/no go process based on value proposition analysis). The lesson is that innovation idea generation and decision is not a random activity. It is not informal; it should be strategic. Once ideas—new ministries, products, services, methods, or processes—are decided upon, they go into the "idea factory" where each goes through a development cycle that includes such things as building a business case for the idea; research and development; building a prototype or pilot to see how the process, product, ministry, or service would work; testing; and further review and analysis that involves such things as a market test. Typically, between each of these steps, there is a review to assure milestones and metrics are being achieved. (Note that if metrics are not being achieved, the organization is in a position to stop the project and refocus its resources on another idea in the pipeline.) This is a continuing process until the idea is ready for launch. Successful ideas thus far within the idea factory then proceed to pilot and final product launch.

Launch is considered the output of the innovation model. Notice that even after process output—launch—there is still the important step of results management. This involves evaluation of how the product (ministry) is being received by customers (members of the community, congregation, future disciples), and working to build acceptance and use.

The lesson that we gain from studying the Tucker model is that it gives a graphic view of how one might adapt a proven model to another context. Further, Tucker emphasizes five key principles:

1. Innovation must be approached as a disciplined process
2. Innovation must be approached comprehensively (all organizations in the church should participate)
3. Innovation must include an organized, systematic, and continual search for new opportunities
4. Innovation must be directed from the top and involve the total enterprise (organization)
5. Innovation must be customer-centered[14]

If we were to take the learning from Tucker's model and propose a simple model for church leaders to consider, I would propose figure 11.2. As noted in the Tucker model, most innovation processes are also built on the idea of progressing through stages and evaluating learning, performance, and associated data to decide if the idea or project should be continued or discontinued. That is one of the benefits of a formal innovation process. You have the benefit of stopping a project early and redirecting resources if performance information from the business case or prototype phase indicate that the objective cannot be met. As such, there is a formal go/no go decision phase at designated points in the process. I will discuss this below.

The stage gate process is a method of guiding the organization's new products, ministries, or processes through five main stages. For example, typical stages are as follows, after there is an idea generation phase. (Idea generation is the step where the organization looks to discover new ministry opportunities. This can be done by conducting community research or brainstorming ideas through methods such as mind maps and brainstorming.)

Stage 1: Scoping: In this stage, the team evaluates the ministry idea or church process improvement to determine its scope. They also try to identify whether the idea is practical and sustainable in the community they serve. This can be done using a tool called SWOT (strengths, weaknesses, opportunities, and threats) analysis. See the resource section at the end of the chapter for details on how to conduct a SWOT analysis.

Stage 2: Build value proposition: At this stage, the organization builds a case for the benefits to be gained from the innovation. For example, is it worth doing the innovation project? Will there be positive impact? Do we have or have access to resources to get it done? Once there is affirmation, a project plan is prepared.[15]

Stage 3: Design and development: This is where the team starts working on the plan to achieve the innovation developed in stage 2. The output of this stage is a prototype or pilot program (make something that works that is similar to the innovation idea that was generated). Critical at this stage is working the plan in a SMART perspective (specific, measurable, achievable, realistic, and time-bound).

Stage 4: Testing and validation: The prototype or pilot program is tested (sometimes multiple times), and feedback and problem information are collected to improve the prototype or pilot program.

Stage 5: Product/process launch or kickoff: This includes followup with the user or customer on acceptance, performance data, and potential improvement opportunities.

In summary, figure 11.2 gives a graphical representation of a simplified model for an implementation and innovation model by using the stage gate process. Yet a key point, as noted above, at each stage is a review and analysis to decide if the value proposition is still achievable. This decision diamond or stage gate is used to determine if the team can still achieve its objectives, if it needs more resources, if it needs to change strategies, or if it can keep moving forward.

Figure 11.2. Innovation Stage Gate Process with Decision Diamonds

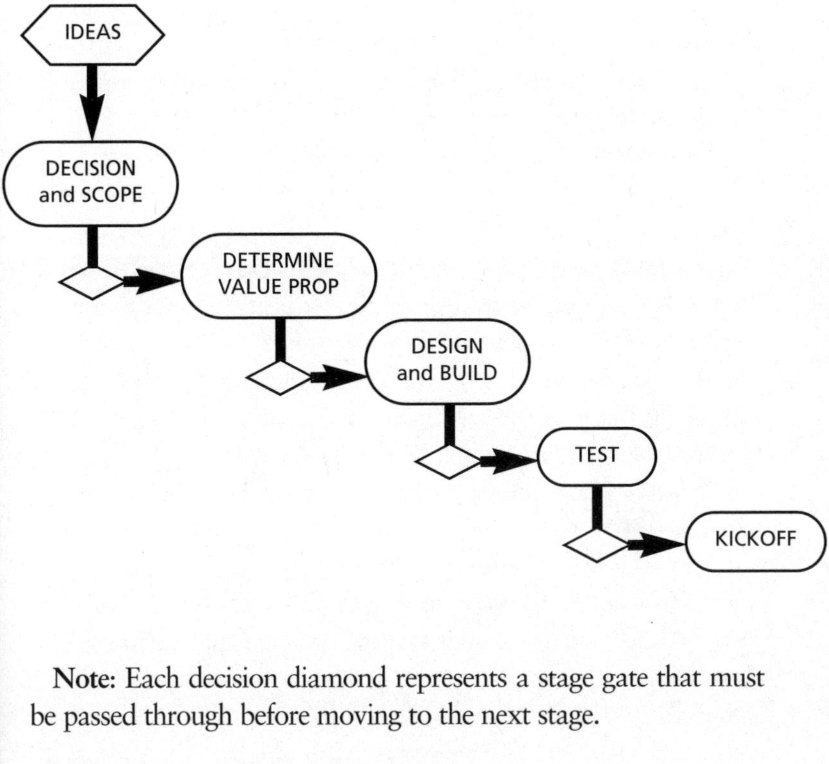

Note: Each decision diamond represents a stage gate that must be passed through before moving to the next stage.

Conclusion

An innovation culture is a requirement for the church today. Kenneth H. Carter Jr., a bishop in the United Methodist Church, and Audrey Warren, a pastor in Miami, affirm this point as they write about a church movement called Fresh Expressions. Fresh Expressions is a form of church that exists specifically for reaching people who don't already go to church, those who have given up on church, or those who have other things to do instead of church. To reach these groups of people—no one solution fits all—we as pastoral leaders must be innovative in worship and evangelism. As Carter and Warren point out, "Meanwhile our cultural landscape is clearly shifting, and we should consider a variety of strategies in response. While the need for new church starts is urgent in the United States, there are cultural and ecclesial shifts afoot that move us toward a new language and a bolder vision."[16]

To achieve this objective requires innovation.

Notes

1. Melinda Emerson, "12 Bible Verses Every Small Business Owner Needs," HuffPost, April 15, 2012, https://www.huffpost.com/entry/small-business-owner-bible_b_1426541.html.

2. Scott D. Anthony, "Innovation Is a Discipline, Not a Cliché," Harvard Business Review, May 30, 2012, https://hbr.org/2012/05/four-innovation-misconceptions.

3. Martin Luenendonk, "The Innovation Process: Definition, Models, Tips," Cleverism, January 22, 2017, https://www.cleverism.com/innovation-process-definition-models-tips/.

4. "Innovation key to church growth," Faith & Leadership, January 3, 2011, https://www.faithandleadership.com/innovation-key-church-growth.

5. Ibid.

6. Larry Osborne, "4 Ways Your Church Can Be Innovative," *Outreach*, January 16, 2017, http://www.outreachmagazine.com/features/21106-church-innovation.html.

7. This list comes from Brian Dodd's article, "20 Current Trends in Innovation Pastors and Church Leaders Should Know,"

https://briandoddonleadership.com/2015/02/14/20-current-trends-in-innovation-pastors-and-church-leaders-should-know/.

8. Ibid.

9. William J. Holstein, "Five Gates to Innovation," Strategy+Business, March 1, 2010, https://www.strategy-business.com/article/00021.

10. Gary P. Pisano, "You Need an Innovation Strategy," *Harvard Business Review*, June 2015, https://hbr.org/2015/06/you-need-an-innovation-strategy.

11. Rebecca M. Henderson and Cate Reavis, "Corning Incorporated: The Growth and Strategy Council," MITSloan, Revised April 15, 2009, https://mitsloan.mit.edu/LearningEdge/CaseDocs/08-056.Corning.GSC.Henderson.pdf.

12. "Accelerate the Evaluation and Maturity of Innovative Ideas: The Innovation Funnel," The DeSai Group, http://www.desai.com/our-approach/innovation-funnel.php.

13. Robert B. Tucker, "Innovation: the new core competency," *Strategy & Leadership* 29 no. 1 (February 1, 2001): 11-14, https://www.emeraldinsight.com/doi/abs/10.1108/10878570110694616.

14. Robert B. Tucker, *Driving Growth Through Innovation: How Leading Firms Are Transforming Their Futures* (San Francisco: Berrett-Koehler Publishers, 2009), 3.

15. For a thorough study of project planning in the church, see *Managing Ministry Projects*, written by Vincent Howell and published by Judson Press.

16. Kenneth H. Carter Jr. and Audrey Warren, *Fresh Expressions: A New Kind of Methodist Church for People Not in Church* (Nashville: Abingdon Press, 2017), 4.

Resources

Books
Anthony, Scott D. *The Little Black Book of Innovation: How It Works, How to Do It*. Brighton, MA: Harvard Business Review Press, 2017.

Buzan, Tony. *Mind Map Mastery: The Complete Guide to Learning and Using the Most Powerful Thinking Tool in the Universe*. London: Watkins Publishing, 2018.

Kaptein, Arthur, et al. *Ultimate Brainstorming: The Facilitator's Toolbox to Great Brainstorming*. CreateSpace, 2014.

Towns, Elmer, Ed Stetzer, and Warren Bird. *11 Innovations in the Local Church: How Today's Leaders Can Learn, Discern and Move into the Future*. Ventura, CA: Regal, 2007.

Articles

Anthony, Scott D. "Innovation Is a Discipline, Not a Cliché."

Burnett, Kristoffer. "Church SWOT Analysis-A Comprehensive Guide," https://spreadsheetsforbusiness.com/church-swot-analysis/. Harvard Business Review. May 30, 2012. https://hbr.org/2012/05 /four-innovation-misconceptions.

Henderson, Rebecca M. and Cate Reavis. "Corning Incorporated: The Growth and Strategy Council." MITSloan. Revised April 15, 2009. https://mitsloan.mit.edu/LearningEdge/CaseDocs/08-056.Corning.GSC.Henderson.pdf.

Vaters, Karl. "Adapt Or Die: 6 Steps to Becoming an Innovative Church." Christianity Today. August 17, 2015. https://www.christianitytoday.com/karl-vaters/2015/august/adapt-or-die-six-steps-to-start-becoming-innovative-church.html.

CHAPTER 12

Project Management

Projects are a part of the work of ministry in any local congregation. They range from updating the parsonage when a new pastor is called to developing a new ministry to grow youth programs, from hosting a holiday meal for the homeless to planning programs during the Advent season. Yet, many times, we do not call this work a project, and, as a result, how they are managed varies within the congregational setting.

A project is a temporary endeavor undertaken to create a unique ministry for the community and God's people. It has a definite beginning and end—hence temporary—and seeks to be a different ministry as compared to other ministries—for example, a church puts on a dinner to feed the homeless as compared to a fundraising project to provide scholarships to community youth. If ministry is viewed as a project, then church work will closely align with the concept of project management. Viewed this way—whether we call it a program, event, or activity—if it is planned, organized, and executed as a project, the church organization is in a much better position to achieve its objective, make use of its people's gifts, and manage fruitful ministries with its limited resources.

Most church projects have a goal, a timeline, a budget, and a team of people to do the work. As such, applying the concept of project management in the local church has the potential to provide some important benefits. Project management practitioners frequently cite a number of benefits of using this concept in the church, according to Northern Ireland's official website for business advice and guidance:

- Reduces the chance of a project failing
- Ensures project quality and ensures that results meet requirements and expectations
- Allows church volunteers to serve in various areas of ministry and increases efficiency both with the project and within the church
- Makes things simpler and easier for the church staff with a single point of contact running the overall project
- Encourages consistent communications among church staff and project team
- Keeps costs, time of completion, and resources on a budget[1]

Theologically, there are two imperatives for applying project management in the church. First, Scripture teaches us that there are projects that are done for the Lord. The classic example from Genesis is when God gave Noah the project to build the ark. This project had time constraints, requirements, and a plan. We also know that the project was managed successfully in that Scripture specifies that the ship withstood the floods for more than 150 days (Genesis 7:24) and that "Noah did everything exactly as God commanded him" (Genesis 6:22, CEB).

The second imperative in Scripture is that we, as church leaders, equip God's people for the work of ministry (Ephesians 4:12). Economic and social challenges from the past few years have placed strain on resources in local churches. Therefore, local churches must be good stewards of the resources they are committed to managing. It is vital that we utilize all available tools that will help result in effective leadership in the church. Project management tools can help church leaders do their work more efficiently. In short, even in the church, we must learn to execute the work of the church effectively as we implement ministries that serve the people of God. Applying project management in the context of the church is one way to achieve that result. The project management process can be visualized as shown in figure 12.1.

Figure 12.1. Project Life Cycle

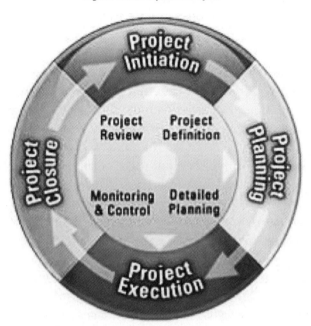

How Churches Can Start Using Project Management

Each church project has four phases:

1. Initiation: In the initiation phase, the scope of the ministry work is defined. It is at this phase where the project manager begins to recruit a project team.

2. Planning: The planning phase is critical and involves outlining the activities, tasks, dependencies, resources, budget, and timeline required to execute the project. In addition, risks are identified and contingency plans are agreed upon.

3. Execution: The execution phase is where most of the work on the project gets done by the project team. During this phase, the project manager and team meet, monitor, and control project tasks to assure that expected outcomes are achieved. Once the ministry event is complete, the project team is ready to move to the closure and evaluation phase.

4. Closure and Evaluation: This is where the project manager, team, congregational leadership, and pastor review how well the project was done. In a project closure and evaluation meeting, the team considers what went well, what should be done differently in the future, and what lessons they learned for future application or sharing with other project teams in the organization. A colleague who spent more than 30 years in pastoral ministry and served as a seminary professor highlighted that one of the things the church does not do well is conducting an evaluation after a project or event is completed. This could be helped by providing structure in managing projects.[2]

Project Management Examples

This first example highlights how project management can be used in planning a ministry with a tight timeline. During the summer of 2014, one of the congregations that I led was working on our revitalization strategy, and members of the group suggested the idea of a "family fun festival" for the community. The idea was to reach out to the community as we prepared to kick off children's Sunday school in September. The project proposal was discussed and approved by the administrative board. One of our leaders, who indicated she had project management experience from her workplace, volunteered to be project manager. Other members volunteered to be on the team. The first project meetings were scheduled, and the objective was agreed upon with the initial project team. Subtasks were developed, documented, and assigned to subtask leaders. For example, subtask leaders were assigned equipment setup, food, communication and outreach, Bible stories, game planning, and so on.

The project manager, along with the subtask leaders, then documented the final project plan and schedule and began weekly meetings based on a seven-week planning and execution phase. These meetings, each beginning with prayer, defined the schedule and a list of project action items for follow-up. The project was executed successfully even though there was a limited time frame. When there's a limited time frame for planning, the work of the project manager is critical. For example, when the vendor for a particular game we needed to rent was not available, the team quickly developed a contingency plan. This is one of the benefits of the structured approach to project management. By meeting at scheduled times and with a plan of execution, when issues arise they are made visible quickly so that project team members can react quickly.

For this church project, the plan was to hold the festival on a Saturday. Community attendance and feedback were positive, and the congregation was energized to repeat the project. A celebration of the work that the Lord had done in our midst was scheduled for the following Tuesday. We were blessed that almost 40 percent of the congregation attended to share their ideas for doing the project again in 2016.

A second case study involves the church and community resources. A member with a passion for community health education had an idea for a project that would raise the church's and community's awareness of heart disease in women. After sharing the idea, training on project management fundamentals was provided. The team then presented the project idea—"The Westside 'Go Red for Women' Tea"—and it was approved. The team defined and documented the project objective, timeline, roles, and responsibilities. It also developed a project plan and a meeting plan. The project was ultimately executed in February 2013. From the first event, it took lessons learned—project evaluation—and has since hosted the event successfully in 2014 and 2015.

Critical Features of Project Management

In order to deliver any project on time and within budget, there are some simple yet critical components of successful church project management to remember. As a leader of a church project, you always need to remember the components and follow the basics of successful project implementation and delivery. Here is a list of the key components to help you better understand the fundamentals of good project planning and management.

■ Make sure that the requirements and goal for your project are clearly written down in detail, so everyone involved in the project (team and leaders of the church) understands what the project is trying to achieve and by when.

■ Project management is about working as a team (it's not individual-focused). Select people with passion for the project who can work together.

■ Always set measureable goals and objectives.

■ You must take the time to document your plan and schedule, including all tasks that need to be done, by whom, and by when (start and finish dates).

■ Good communication is essential.

■ In your planning, keep an eye on things that might cause the project to get off schedule or potentially fail. This is often called risk planning and therefore requires a contingency plan if these issues arise.

Conclusion

The essence of church project management is that it helps us live the Word: God gave different roles, responsibilities, and functions in the church "for the equipping of the saints for the work of ministry, for the edifying of the body of Christ" (Ephesians 4:12, NKJV). As such, church project management can be viewed as a set of tools that can be used by the lay and pastoral leaders in managing God's work in ministerial projects. For a more in-depth resource on church project management, see *Managing Projects in Ministry*.

Notes

1. www.nibusinessinfo.co.UK.

2. Vincent Wyatt Howell, "Using Project Management in the Church," The Upper New York Conference of the United Methodist Church, March 7, 2016, http://www.unyumc.org/news/article/project-management-in-church.

Resources

Book

Howell, Vincent Wyatt. *Managing Projects in Ministry*. Valley Forge, PA: Judson Press, 2017. Along with the book there are online resources, such as templates for project planning, project evaluation, and other tasks.

Online Tool

Project Management Software. Capterra. https://www.capterra.com/-project-management-software/. Some of these applications come at no cost.

CHAPTER 13

Wisdom from Pastors and Church Leaders Who Earned the MBA

As was mentioned earlier, a number of schools now offer pastors and ministers the opportunity to pursue joint Master of Divinity/Master of Business Administration degrees. Furthermore, many local small, large, public, and private colleges and universities provide opportunities for students to earn an MBA in online, evening, weekend, or executive degree programs. One colleague also mentioned that, because her work setting was nonprofit, the university provided reduced tuition to help offset the cost.

With the changes to ministry context that require pastors to have a broader set of leadership tools, pastors who are earning or have earned the MBA as part of their leadership training have put themselves in the position to apply innovative and creative ministries as they lead their congregations into the future. We hope the previous chapters have given you insight into how this type of leadership development can be beneficial to your ministry and the calling God has put on your life. As further insight, a Christian university in my geographical area that offers the Master of Divinity and Master of Business Administration degree summarizes the importance this learning can have on a pastor's ministry:

- Understand how to manage and motivate people
- Understand and interpret financial statements
- Learn better financial decision-making
- Learn techniques for getting the word out about your ministry programs

■ Practice strategic planning and decision-making
■ Avoid legal and ethical problems
■ Improve your understanding of the environment in which you operate—how do economic, cultural, technological, and global changes impact your work?

Whether a pastor chooses to pursue an MBA, take MBA courses, complete an executive leadership program offered by a graduate business school, or even use this book as a stepping stone to broaden leadership knowledge beyond a traditional theological degree, that knowledge will be valuable. Therefore, I have asked MBA-degreed pastors to share their wisdom as a way to give insight for those looking to expand their leadership capacity. These pastors come from varied contexts, denominations, geographical locations, and pastoral roles. Special thanks for sharing go to:

Jan Cason, MDiv, MBA, finance manager, George W. Truett Theological Seminary, Baylor University, Waco, Texas

Rev. Rebecca Laird, MDiv, MBA, pastor, Moravia United Methodist Church, Moravia, New York

Rev. Matt Steen, MDiv, MBA, executive pastor, Rancho Murieta Community Church, Rancho Murieta, California

Rev. Lawrence Williams, BSME, MBA, pastor, Higher Purpose Church, Mooresville, North Carolina

Jan Cason

Jan Cason is a lay member who has earned both the Master of Divinity and the MBA. She currently is the finance manager at Baylor University's George W. Truett Theological Seminary in Waco, Texas, a role she has held for more than eight years.

Jan brings a unique perspective to the benefit of earning both the MDiv and MBA for church leaders. Speaking of her calling to ministry, Jan is clear that she has a calling, not to be a pastor, but to be a church administrator. She has grown up in the church since her youth, and the clarity of her call is even evidenced through her service as an administrator for a Baptist association in Abilene, Texas, while she attended college. Upon graduating from college with an accounting degree, Jan eventually was called to serve as the church administrator (including the role of minister of adult education) at Meadowbrook Baptist Church in Waco, Texas. (This position is now called the executive pastor at Meadowbrook.) Jan served in church administration ministry for almost five years. It was this ministry leadership experience that led her to make the decision to pursue and complete seminary training via the Master of Divinity degree at Baylor University's George W. Truett Theological Seminary, an orthodox, evangelical school in the historic Baptist tradition embedded into a major research university.

With a finance and accounting background, and a newly earned Master of Divinity, Jan eventually joined the Seminary at Baylor as the finance manager. As she continued to serve in her local church and community, her colleagues comment that she:

> makes important and significant contributions to the larger Waco community. She is an active member at Meadowbrook Baptist Church where she serves on the budget committee and as the pianist. Jan also serves on the leadership team for the Waco Regional Baptist Association and has been instrumental in keeping Baylor and Truett connected with the churches in this association. She is president of the board for "You Set Me Free Ministries" and continues to lead an important ministry in the community —"Widow and Widowers Grief Study Group." In her work with the larger community, Jan reflects the very best of what it means to be *Pro Ecclesia, Pro Texana*.[1]

Relative to ministry, Jan is rooted in the importance of following your passion and where you see God leading you. This is clearly seen in her ministry. When she and her husband were stationed in England, a group of four couples (including Jan) noticed that there was no evangelical ministry (only Roman Catholic and Anglican) in the area. As a result, Jan and her colleagues (two civilians and two military) organized the Amesbury Baptist Church back in the early 1990s. This church plant continues to thrive today.

When I asked her about the decision to pursue the MBA, she stated that her focus was applying the learning to her ministry of administration. She said, "I did not get an MBA to go into the corporate world; my focus was [to] expand my ability to expand the ministry of Jesus Christ."

Because of Jan's combined experience in congregational leadership as a church administrator (practical), church planting, and her finance background, the dean of the seminary asked Jan to develop and teach a practical elective course for Baylor's joint MDiv/MBA program. The course, The Business of Ministry, "is designed for church leaders to study church business concepts and basic administrative practices in order to enhance the vision and ministry of the church. Major emphases include constitution and bylaws, policies and procedures, financial processes, budgets, personnel issues, tax and legal issues, risk management, facilities management, church debt, social media, personal finances, donor issues, and stewardship philosophies."[2] This is a course Jan teaches each spring, and it has continued to be an important elective for the past eight years.

During May 2018, Cason, along with Truett Seminary's Associate Dean for Academic Affairs and Professor of Christian Ministry and Church Music, Dr. Terry York, traveled to Ghana at the invitation of Dora Bortey, DMin, the founder and director of L.I.F.E. (Living For El-Shaddai) Ministries, an organization that focuses on reaching children and teenagers for Jesus Christ, in

Africa. In Ghana, Cason and her colleague twice facilitated a two-day pastors' seminar entitled "The Church: Responsible and Worshiping," once at Calvary Baptist Church in Accra and once at Living Waters Assemblies of God Church in Kumasi. Cason presented on church administration and business in the church setting to over fifty participants, mostly local Baptist pastors; the leadership knowledge exchange and expertise shared was warmly welcomed and generated many questions.[3] International teaching of this type of joint theological and business administration leadership asserts the broad importance of leadership capacity developed in the global church.

When I asked Jan the benefits of pastors obtaining an MBA degree, Jan highlighted several key points:

■ Helps broaden leadership perspective and vision

■ Helps to build leadership integrity based on building a broad set of skills relevant to the importance of policies and procedures put in place for the protection of our stewardship mandate

■ Helps build strong church managerial skills—helps the pastor broaden her or his view of the world and its intersection with ministry

■ By learning of the role of pastoral/church leadership and business acumen, pastors gain more confidence in leading not only the business side of the church, but also leadership related to pastoral staff and overall church and community communication

■ Pastors are better equipped to steward God's money—"Pastors are the executors for the spending of the resources provided by our congregations. As such, they control their money and their worship ministry expectations. The better pastoral leaders know how to steward God's money, the better we can build integrity of ministry."

■ Helps pastors better relate to businesspeople in the community. As such, the more the pastor knows about business the more he or she can help minister to that segment of the community.

In summary, Jan Cason reasons that there will be a shift in church leadership structure in the future. Namely, there will be more of a bi-vocational pastor structure, where leadership skills will be critical to create a church that seeks to reach those outside the church from different demographics. (Cason is also working with Baylor on a Lilly Foundation research grant on how to develop future leaders for this paradigm shift.) Thus, she leaves an important thought on the importance of pastoral leadership skills necessary for leading the church in the future: "Whether you are pastoring a small church or a large church, you will either do the job or be responsible for the job." Strong church management skills are a requirement.

Notes

1. "Jan Cason," Baylor University, https://www.baylor.edu/hr/doc.php/193249.pdf.

2. "The Business of Ministry: Lead 7V21," Baylor University, Spring 2014, https://www.ats.edu/uploads/resources/current-initiatives/economic-challenges-facing-future-ministers/financial-literacy-programs/baylor-business-of-ministry-syllabus.pdf.

3. "Truett Travels to Ghana," Baylor University, June 7, 2018, https://www.baylor.edu/truett/news.php?action=story&story=199532.

Rev. Rebecca Laird

Rev. Laird is an ordained minister in the United Methodist Church. She has served as a pastor in the upstate area of New York State. Having served in pastoral ministry for twelve years, she earned the Master of Divinity degree from Asbury Theological Seminary in Wilmore, Kentucky, in 2006. Her ministry and pastoral leadership have been in both rural and urban settings, including at times pastoring three-point, two-point, and single congregations. This ministry has also included church planting, where she was led to plant a non-traditional congregation in Syracuse, New York, called "The

ROAD Church." The ROAD stands for Relational, Open to all, Affirming and Diverse. This style church is what Rebecca considers a fresh expression of church—it seeks to reach those outside the church, those who need another approach to church, those who seem to have fallen through the cracks in society, and those who need a hand. A recent newspaper article describes the church as the "New face of the United Methodist Church." The ROAD does not conduct church in the traditional Sunday service model—they minister through such means as hosting open mic nights, doing food and clothing giveaways (think sandwich giveaway on a busy street corner), communion and prayer in the community (again, where people gather in community setting, including on downtown streets), and the occasional craft fair on Sunday where several dozen people discuss everything from Scriptures to atheism.[1]

As the ministry continued to grow, the church plant eventually was able to acquire meeting space that included a community space, complete with a fully-operating cafe area called "Wholely Grounds," a venture that help sustain the ministry by offering food and drinks for suggested donations. The ROAD also meets during the week at community gathering places (the idea is to take church where the people are instead of expecting people to always come to the church building). These faith locations include sports pubs, grilles, cafes, and movie theaters on Thursday nights at 6 p.m. so that people can chat openly about their faith and life stories over food and drinks.

It was in this ministry setting that Rev. Laird considered what management and leadership strategy would be required to sustain this type of ministry model. When she first started this venture, it was partially funded through denominational grants and area church donations. As such, she had a keen desire to understand the finance side of such a new start-up. Note that she uses the term new start-up. Whether the new start-up is a church, nonprofit, or technology venture, there are still requirements for long-term (and short-term) sustainability, including financial management, strategic planning, and operations management.

Having pastored other churches that struggled with finances and knowing that a new venture of this sort needed a different church management and leadership model, Rebecca stated that this was the reason she felt earning an MBA would broaden leadership skills that could be translated to the church. As such, some of her favorite courses focused on new venture start-ups and creating new businesses. These are things she felt would help with new church plants and the required innovation for the church of the future. In addition, Rev. Laird stated that coursework in finance was a great help making good, sound decisions based on data instead of emotion, developing strategy, and understanding a broader business approach to organizational strategy, i.e., seeing how other types of organizations do strategic management and what can be applied to the church.

Rev. Laird completed her MBA at the University of Rochester's Simon Business School (Rochester, New York) in June 2018. When I asked her for thoughts on why she would recommend MBA coursework for today's pastors, the wisdom Rebecca shared includes the following:

■ Since MBA-type leadership courses are not typically taught in traditional seminary, some pastors have learned leadership lessons from the "school of hard knocks." This type of hands-on learning is valuable, but focused learning is also valuable, especially when you consider the learning that is gained through shared experiences and group learning in a business school setting.

■ MBA programs allow students to learn the business concept of competition. Some church leaders don't like to look at church as being in competition with business, community events, and any other event or activity taking place in the community. But competition is anything that prevents people from coming to church. As pastors we need to understand competition, culture, and strategy to compete with the world around us.

■ In the culture we live in today, we need to find creative ways to reach younger generations (in MBA terms this is marketing). In business school, this is a fundamental that is taught.

■ Having an MBA helps put pastors in a position to feel more comfortable navigating outside the traditional church space. That is the space where members are in their world of work. Understanding their paradigm helps us to understand them better.

■ The MBA gives pastors a broader skill set. The church is a community-based organization, just like a small business. It just has a different purpose and calling. Nonetheless, the church is still a people-based organization, and the pastor must be able to manage effectively. The MBA skill set helps pastors lead in common church and community language, thereby being able to interface and lead in the community in a more expansive way.

On a personal level for the pastor, the church model of the future may move further away from local churches being the sole sustainers of their pastors' livelihoods. A number of churches are not able to pay a full-time salary to a pastor who is supporting a family. But this should not deter a person from fulfilling God's call to ministry. By having theological training combined with the MBA, pastors have a strong theological foundation and also management education to enhance their effectiveness in ministry, business, non-profit, and public sector careers. The result is that pastors can take care of their families and are in a position to provide strong leadership, no matter the size of the church.

Note

1. Katrina Tulloch, "The ROAD: Redefining faith traditions one peanut butter sandwich at a time," Syracuse.com, October 28, 2015, https://www.syracuse.com/entertainment/index.ssf/2015/10

/the_road_redefining_church_traditions_one_peanut_butter_sand-wich_at_a_time.html.

Rev. Matt Steen

Rev. Matt Steen is Executive Pastor at Rancho Murieta Community Church (RMCC), in the Sacramento, California, area. The church is part of the Christian and Missionary Alliance. Matt grew up in the Baltimore, Maryland, area, and during his ministry Matt has served as a youth pastor, a church planter, and an executive pastor before joining the RMCC team in his current role. His twenty years of ministry have included planting a church in Baltimore, eight years as youth pastor, and consulting with pastors and church planters. Having received his call to ministry early in life, Matt majored in youth ministry when pursuing his bachelor's degree.

When I caught up with Matt to discuss his life in ministry, how he chose the educational route of both MDiv and MBA degrees, and the benefits he sees for other pastors in attaining MBA learning, he was on his way to a preaching engagement. Quickly in our conversation I could tell he has a passion for sharing the word of God and a spirit for ministry innovation. Matt credits this to a key ministry developmental opportunity—while he was in college, he was fortunate to intern at a church that focused on leadership development. The church, he says, helped build in him a ministry-focused entrepreneurial spirit. After college, he worked in college youth ministry, missions leadership, community transformation, and church marketing and strategy in addition to serving in the church.

I asked Matt how he came to choose his educational direction. His response was that, because of the entrepreneurial spirit formed during his youth ministry studies, the innovative ministry projects he was involved with, and with the nudging of the Holy Spirit on his life, the choice of the joint MDiv/MBA route seemed natural (note that Matt did a joint MDiv/MBA program as compared to completing the MDiv first and the MBA later in life). His choice of school was the George W. Truett School of Theology at Baylor University.

During the pursuit of his studies, Matt also served in the roles of Director of Campus Operations/Director of Connections at Harris Creek Baptist Church in Waco, Texas. His work experience coupled with studies translated into a very practical operations management orientation to ministry and church leadership. He describes this role, saying, "I spend my time working behind the scenes, coordinating teams of ministry volunteers, and leading large church projects. If I'm doing things right, people won't see me doing ministry. They'll see lots of well-trained, empowered ministry teams and individuals serving with their talents and unique gifts, all in service to Christ." I used the operations management nomenclature in the above description because Matt said his typical ministry week included coordinating campus operations, managing volunteers, troubleshooting facility and personnel issues, planning large projects, and implementing our church vision through leadership teams. (These are all things needed in the church, as we discussed in earlier chapters.)

In discussing why did Rev. Steen decided to earn a joint MDiv/MBA degree, he replied that his "entrepreneurial wiring" made him a non-traditional seminary student because he likes to start new ventures and innovative projects. For example, he is the cofounder of a ministry company called Chemistry Staffing, which he described as an organization that has a mission to "help churches and potential staff members make healthy connections. Chemistry Staffing's process has one goal: a long-term, healthy fit for both the church and the staff member. Great things happen when the right leadership is in place in a local church . . . lives are changed and churches thrive." In past years, he has started other ministry consulting firms. According to Steen, "The MBA part made a lot of sense. It allows the pursuit of ministry on a different track—not purely academic but ministry action-oriented, focused on leadership coaching, navigating staff transition."

Looking back over this educational journey in light of his current and past ministry roles, Matt highlights the following:

■ The MBA has helped build on his entrepreneurial spirit within the ministry (we always need to be thinking of ways to innovate in ministry for the context where we serve).

■ The MBA helped him to understand people whom he would minister to. This included the ability to work with business leaders and people who operate in a corporate culture. The MBA gives unique insight into what this group in some of our congregations value and what shapes them. There can be new lessons in leadership to learn from these members.

■ The study of organizational communications helps pastoral leaders to understand the people better. Furthermore, speaking and doing a business presentation are different than preaching in a seminary context. But the blending of preaching skills and business presentations helps us as pastors and preachers be better communicators.

■ MBA skills help with decision analysis. It will provide knowledge to help decision makers decide, "does the data really support pursuing this building expansion project or not? Should we be doing something more sustainable?"

■ There is a lack of business sense in the church world. Yet we are called to steward God's resources; we must be able to understand the financial side.

■ For pastoral leaders, it is valuable to have a different set of leadership disciplines than traditionally taught; it adds leadership practicality and depth.

■ In summary, Matt Steen felt that a key piece of learning that comes from his joint Master of Divinity/Master of Business Administration is the "ability to exegete the congregation."

Rev. Lawrence Williams

Pastor Lawrence Williams is the founding pastor of Higher Purpose Church in Mooresville, North Carolina, a congregation affiliated with the Assemblies of God denomination. Lawrence planted this church back in 2005. The congregation is predominantly African American with a focus on becoming multiethnic.

As a bi-vocational pastor, Pastor Lawrence also worked in corporate America as an engineer, most recently as Product Line Process Excellence Manager at a major technology company. As such, Lawrence is a pastor who came into ministry with an MBA (he is a graduate of the Wake Forest University School of Business in Winston Salem, NC).

Having been heavily involved in youth and adult ministry at an early age, Lawrence accepted God's call to preach and was licensed to preach in the Church of God in Christ (COGIC) at the Word of Faith Church in Elmira, New York. There he served as an assistant minister, Director of Finance, and Minister of Music. After a work-related relocation, he served in ministry at the Christian Outreach of the Piedmont Church in Statesville, North Carolina. It was from this ministry that in 2005 he founded what is now known as Higher Purpose Church, a congregation that began as a Bible study that met at a hotel meeting room. Upon building the new plant, Pastor Lawrence was credentialed as an ordained minister with the General Council of the Assemblies of God. From its early beginnings, the church has grown into a strong community and family-focused ministry that includes community outreach ministry, a married couples ministry, a kids ministry whose goal is to partner with parents to lead the next generation to become fully devoted followers and "Change Agents for Christ," men's ministries, and growth groups (their terminology for small groups). In the Higher Purpose context, these small groups offer the opportunity to more wholly experience God through close relationships as members play and pray together, encourage and help one another, and study and live out God's Word together.

As a pastor who is described as a gifted teacher of the Word, an entrepreneurial-oriented leader who encourages and instructs others to create their own businesses (as part of his ministry, he has presented numerous seminars on Money Management and Church Finances), and one who brings biblically based, life-changing principles to everyday living, he brings a unique perspective to pastors seeking MBA knowledge. The three points of wisdom he shares for pastoral leaders are as follows:

■ "I can't imagine doing ministry without the leadership development provided by the MBA. Even though I earned the degree while working in the corporate world, the learning has fostered and helped provide insight into current-day church leadership requirements—things such as how to market the church in a society that is market driven, organizational behavior, leadership, and the importance of systems management."[1]

■ "The MBA provides a broader leadership perception that is critical for the church paradigm. For example, I sit on the North Carolina Assemblies of God district leadership board. When we consider pastoral leadership requirements for the future, there are key focal points—the call to preach (heart and soul of ministry) and a systems orientation to leadership (how the leader's skills help impact the overall effectiveness and fruitfulness of the church). Leadership therefore is important as we seek to help the body grow through—worship systems linking such components as the praise team, financial systems, human systems (assimilation of new people into the body, connecting people to ministry service, transformation from visitor to committed disciples), strategic vision (Where is God leading us as a congregation, team, small group?), and the required systems for evaluation (What works? What should we change? How can we do a better job in serving the Lord and [God's] people?)?"

■ "MBA programs, particularly the one I attended, seek to equip students with a strategic, global perspective on business, and to sharpen leadership ability to approach challenges from a variety of perspectives. With that said, innovation and innovative leadership is at the heart. In our ministry, innovation is a huge part of how I view my leadership role—it's like a value. In ministry, we need to always be looking to see how learning can apply to the world changing around us. As the church, we must adapt to keep the gospel out front and relevant. I read somewhere that society changes every three years, but the church changes every fifty years. The MBA program challenges us to keep growing in leadership— even we as pastors need to keep up with the megatrends coming and determine how we adapt—with new skills, what new things we need—to be able to go where is God leading us."

Note

1. Systems approach is based on the generalization that everything is interrelated and interdependent. A system is composed of related and dependent elements which, when in interaction, form a unitary whole. A system is simply an assemblage or combination of things or parts forming a complex whole. From a church management perspective, in the systems approach, attention is paid to the overall effectiveness of the system, i.e., the total church operation, rather than the effectiveness of the subsystems, i.e., one department, such as the choir or the trustee board.

APPENDIX 1

Sample Listing of Schools That Offer Joint MDiv/MBA Degree Programs

Baylor University, https://www.baylor.edu/business/mba/index.php?id=93938

Eastern University, https://www.eastern.edu/academics/graduate-programs/mdivmba-social-impact

Emory University, http://candler.emory.edu/academics/degrees/business/index.html

Gardner-Webb University, https://gardner-webb.edu/academic-programs-and-resources/colleges-and-schools/business/graduate-programs/dual-masters-degrees/business-divinity/index

Harvard University, https://hds.harvard.edu/academics/degree-programs/dual-degrees

Howard University, http://divinity.howard.edu/academics_master_business_admin.html

Louisville Presbyterian Theological Seminary, http://www.lpts.edu/academics/degrees-programs/dual-degrees/theology-and-business

Mercer University, https://business.mercer.edu/programs/atlanta-mba/mba-mdiv/

North Park University, https://www.northpark.edu/seminary/academics/dual-degrees/master-of-divinity-and-mba-or-mna/mdiv-and-mba-program-requirements/

Palm Beach Atlantic University, http://catalog.pba.edu/preview_program.php?catoid=32&poid=5324&returnto=2440

Samford University, https://www.samford.edu/business/joint-degree-programs

Seattle Pacific University, http://spu.edu/academics/school-of-business-and-economics/graduate-programs/dual-degrees

Vanderbilt University, https://business.vanderbilt.edu/mba/curriculum/joint-degrees/

Yale University, https://som.yale.edu/programs/joint-degrees/mba-mdiv-or-mar-yale-divinity-school

Sample Financial Management Policy

CHURCH OF FINANCIAL MANAGEMENT

<u>I. POLICY</u>
Each ministry team of <u>(church name)</u> requires financial resources in order to perform its role in the ministry of the church mission of making disciples, teaching, and serving the community.

Each ministry team leader is responsible for ensuring that their teams manage financial resources in a spiritual, efficient, and cost-effective manner.

Each ministry team leader shall adopt the following principles and responsibilities to ensure sound church financial management.

<u>II. DEFINITIONS</u>
The term "ministry team" refers to the common terms typically used by the church, such as committee, board, or auxiliary. The connotation is that a team works together, cares for each other, and seeks to achieve its common goal for Christ. All church organizations are considered ministry teams, e.g., choir, Trustees, human resources, etc.

<u>III. PRINCIPLES</u>
Principle 1: A budget must be established to provide a tool to:

1. evaluate resources necessary to achieve a ministry team and church goals and objectives,

2. measure current financial performance,

3. discover significant transaction errors, and

4. detect substantial changes in circumstances or church business conditions.

Principle 2: A budget must be realistic, reasonable, and attainable.

Principle 3: A budget must be based on a thorough analysis that includes:

1. a clear identification of the budget's purpose to the ministry team's mission, goals, and objectives,

2. a comprehensive assessment of the team's financial needs in order to fulfill its goals, and

3. a plan to increase resources or modify goals and objectives, if current resources fall short of meeting church or ministry team needs.

Principle 4: Actual financial results must be compared to the budget on a regular basis to:

1. detect changes in conditions related to the church or the community environment,

2. discover transaction errors,

3. measure financial performance,

4. ensure unnecessary costs are being avoided,

5. ensure that expenditures are reasonable and necessary to accomplish the team or church goals, and

6. ensure that transactions are adequately supported.

Principle 5: When actual financial results vary significantly from the budget, a leader must:

a. determine the cause,

b. evaluate the activity, and
c. take corrective action.

Principle 6: Ministry teams must operate within their budget. Where expenditures exceed budget (or are expected to exceed), justification for such excess must be provided before proceeding. Additionally the ministry team must develop a formal plan to eliminate deficits generated.

Principle 7: All expenditures must comply with all relevant church policies, rules, and regulations.

Principle 8: Each ministry team must evaluate the financial consequences before a new activity is started or a current activity is a changed or eliminated. Changes should be reported to the Finance Team Leader.

Principle 9: Each ministry team must ensure that the anticipated benefits are greater than the costs for any planned or ongoing activities.

Principle 10: Each ministry team must provide adequate safeguards to protect against the loss or unauthorized use of church funds or assets.

IV. RESPONSIBILITIES

Section 1: Planning and Budgeting
1. All planning and budgeting must include:
   ■ A mission statement with goals and objectives for each ministry team. This statement should be simple, direct, attainable, and measurable. It must be specific enough to be integrated into the overall planning and budgeting process.

■ A thorough process for identifying, implementing, and evaluating activities and projects required to achieve the ministry team goals which are based on prudent and supportable projections which have taken into account the needs and impact on certain key factors including:

a. attendance, student enrollment (e.g., Sunday school class), participation,

b. supporting and auxiliary services required,

c. space, equipment, and supplies requirements,

d. salaries, benefits, honorariums,

e. anticipated revenue,

f. capital expenditures that are not included in the church budget, and

g. interdependency among ministry teams.

2. Consistent use of proven methods for gathering and analyzing data.

3. Sufficient detail and descriptive narration to clearly portray how all of the ministry team's projects are being financed, including:
■ all funding sources,
■ revenue estimates,
■ major expenditures by category,
■ major assumptions and forecasting methods used,
■ significant changes in current activities, and
■ contingency plans.

In addition, all budget data should be cross-referenced to the ministry team's stated goals and objectives.

1. A cost/expenditure management plan to maximize the resources available to the church.

2. A thorough re-evaluation of all assumptions, analyses, plans, and budgets used in the previous year's planning and budgeting

process. Since goals and objectives may change from year to year, all data feeding into current plans and budgets must be reevaluated each year to ensure that it reflects today's environment.

For further information contact the Church Finance Leader.

Section 2: Monitoring and Evaluating Financial Data

All systems for monitoring and evaluating financial data must include:

1. Monthly financial reports that are appropriate and accurate. These reports must:
   - be clear, concise, and detailed,
   - identify all sources of revenue and expenditure,
   - provide budget verses actual comparisons,
   - clearly identify trends and special areas of concern and highlight exception items.

2. A method for reviewing revenue and expenses at the end of each ledger cycle:
   - If such a review reveals problems or exceptions, these must be addressed in time to take appropriate action before the next cycle ends, and
   - If reporting exceptions continue to occur, control procedures must be implemented to correct the situation.

3. A monthly sampling of financial transactions. The sampling must be large enough to ensure that:
   - the proper full accounting units are being posted to,
   - terms, conditions, and restrictions imposed by University policy or external funding sources are being adhered to,
   - names appearing on salary and benefit transactions are valid and appropriate,
   - salaries reconcile to timesheet records, and
   - other expenditures are appropriate and include adequate supporting documentation.

4. An examination for each significant deviation to determine the cause, including:
- deviations from policies or other church guidelines,
- deliberate decisions to depart from the budget,
- transaction errors, or
- abuse of authority.

5. A method for taking corrective actions, which includes:
- revising plans or budgets to reflect changed circumstances,
- changing or eliminating activities,
- obtaining additional funding,
- modifying goals or objectives,
- correcting transaction errors,
- altering future budget assumptions,
- implementing new control procedures, or
- documenting managerial decisions that depart from the budget.

6. Documentation of the corrective actions, which includes:
- why the variance occurred,
- how the budget was revised,
- what accounts were affected,
- when the actions were taken, and
- who authorized the actions.

Section 3: Analyzing Costs, Benefits, and Risks

The Finance Ministry Team, along with the appropriated ministry team, e.g., Christian Education, must weigh the costs and risks before deciding to significantly add, change, or eliminate activities. This analysis is to be followed with a formal proposal which includes:
- a clear statement of purpose,
- a quantified statement of benefits to the unit, the University, and any outside interests,
- references to previous similar proposals,

■ references to other related activities and to other units that will be affected,

■ a thorough quantification of all direct and indirect costs, FTE counts, space needs, and capital expenditures,

■ anticipated funding sources,

■ potential problems,

■ significant underlying assumptions, and

■ identification and assessment of all financial, service, and organizational risks to the unit and to the University.

Section 4: Safeguarding Church Assets

1. Church assets must be safeguarded from loss or unauthorized use. Adequate safeguards include that:

■ All cash, checks, or cash equivalents collections are deposited on the day they are received.

■ Cash equivalents that cannot be readily identified with a particular ministry team or account must be deposited to the General Account.

■ All cash shortages and excesses must be promptly reported to a Finance Team Leader, who must investigate.

■ All petty cash and change funds must be authorized by the Finance Ministry Team. Once established, only one church member or employee must be responsible for managing such funds, and a second church member or employee must monitor and review the fund to ensure honest and accurate disbursement.

■ A physical inventory of all inventoriable equipment must be conducted at least once per year. All discrepancies must be promptly reported and investigated.

■ Adjustments to asset records must be documented and approved.

■ Access to any forms or computer systems that can be used to alter financial records and/or balances must be restricted to designated persons who require such access to perform their ministry duties in the church. The names of the designated persons shall be approved by the Administrative Council and shall be kept on file by the church secretary.

■ Delinquent account balances must be carefully examined, and all follow-up collection or write-off actions must be completed in a timely manner.

The format of this sample is adapted from "Principles of Financial Management," UCLA, https://www.finance.ucla.edu/corporate-accounting/principles-of-financial -management.

About the Authors

Vincent Howell currently serves as pastor of the Centenary United Methodist Churches in Clemmons, North Carolina. He is the author of *Managing Projects in Ministry*, also published by Judson Press. In addition to his more than twenty years of pastoral experience as a bi-vocational minister, he has applied and taught strategic planning, project management, and business ethics as adjunct professor of management in the graduate school at Elmira College. Having created a church strategic planning workshop, he has taught the concept to local churches and has been a conference speaker on the topic.

Reverend Howell received a Bachelor of Science degree in industrial technology (manufacturing) from North Carolina A&T State University and a Master of Arts in management from Salve Regina University, where he also received the university's 2010 Distinguished Graduate Alumni Award. He is a 1986 graduate of the Colgate Rochester Crozer Divinity School in Rochester, New York, and earned a Doctor of Ministry degree from the Ecumenical Theological Seminary, Detroit, Michigan, in 2013. He and his wife, Carolyn, enjoy spending time with their two grandchildren.

Vincent Howell Jr. is IT Supervisor, business analysis at a major corporation and is a deacon at the First Baptist Church in Murfreesboro, Tennessee. He holds a Bachelor of Science degree in computer science from Tennessee State University and has also earned a Master of Business Administration degree. Over the years, he has participated in local church audio-visual, website development, and transportation ministries. When not participating in various ministries at his church, Vincent and his wife, LaToya, are raising their two young children.